TEACHING PROBLEM SOLVING

an introduction for primary and junior secondary teachers

by

Derek Holton:
Professor of Mathematics, Otago University, New Zealand

Anthony Neyland:
Secondary Teacher, Nelson College, New Zealand

Jim Neyland:
Lecturer in Education, Victoria University, Wellington, New Zealand

Bronwen Thomas:
Primary Teacher, Wakari School, Dunedin, New Zealand

First Published 1999
by KINGSHAM Press
Chichester, West Sussex. U.K

Printed and Bound by St. Richards Press,
Chichester; United Kingdom

British Library Cataloguing in Publication Data
A catalogue record of this book is available from the British Library
Holton, Derek; Neyland, Jim; Neyland, Anthony; Thomas, Bronwen.

ISBN 0-9527912-0-X

Contents

FOREWORD

This book is written for pre- and in-service training of primary and junior secondary teachers. Ideally it will be used as a text for a course which we estimate will last for approximately 20 contact hours or it can be used for individual reading and study. We recommend that teachers will gain more from the experience if they work together in groups during the course.

The text is liberally sprinkled with questions that are both mathematical and pedagogical/philosophical. The latter questions are devised to stimulate teachers' thinking of the issues that we raise. It is these questions that will be enhanced by small group discussions. We should point out at the start, that we don't expect that **every** reader will solve **all** of these problems. Each individual should do what they think is necessary to understand the relevant topic.

Most of the non-mathematical questions are answered sooner or later in the text itself. This is not the case for the mathematical problems. We hope that teachers can solve these for themselves, though, if they have difficulty, they should work with others to produce solutions.

The material in this book is the product of many years of research and teaching experience. All of the problems we have used have been tested on more than one occasion in the classroom. Much of the discussion around these problems has actually taken place in some class at some time.

Of course, it is not possible to anticipate how individuals will react to particular problems. So we may not have provided just the scaffolding that a given individual needs at any precise moment. At this stage teachers will need to discuss their difficulties with each other. It is somewhat difficult to know quite how to teach problem solving using the medium of print. First, as we say later, teaching problem solving can be achieved in a variety of ways depending on many variables. And second, to really help someone's teaching style you have to observe it in action. This part of the process has to be left to the person running the course or the people working with you in your group. However, we have done our best to lay a trail for others to follow but the trail should not be followed slavishly.

The final thing that has to be said is that this is just an **introduction** to the teaching of problem solving. Our aim is to get teachers started. Hence, although we hope that teachers will eventually use a problem solving approach throughout **all** of their mathematics teaching, we only concentrate here in developing expertise in single, unrelated, lessons. Once teachers have gained confidence at this level we hope they will be able to see how to take the next step themselves or we will have had time to write the appropriate sequel to this book.

ACKNOWLEDGEMENTS

We would like to thank Sharron Eade, Irene Goodwin, Lenette Grant and Leanne Kirk for their help in preparing the manuscript for this book. We are also grateful for the many children and teachers we have worked with and the insight they have given us into the learning process.

CHAPTER 1 THE TEDDY BEARS' PICNIC

1. A PROBLEM WITH BUTTONS

Every year at this time, the Teddy Bear's picnic is only two weeks away. Teddy the Bear has read all the good children's story books and knows that he and his family should all go there in matching waistcoats. So Teddy and his wife and their three children go off to Arthur Barnett's to get their gear. They pick out some beautiful red waistcoats each with three blue buttons. But Mrs Bear says she would prefer green ones. The shop assistant says "No worries, we'll have green ones on for you by Friday".

How many green buttons will the shop assistant at Arthur Barnett's have to get for the five bear's waist coats?

Now to you and me this is a simple problem. Five waistcoats, three buttons to a waistcoat, five times three equals fifteen. No trouble at all. The fact is it really isn't a problem at all. We've all be in so many situations like this that the whole process is virtually automatic.

But for most five year olds, who have just come to school, the buttons' problem is a **real** problem. These children have probably never seen anything like this before at all. They have no idea about multiplication and may not even be able to count up to 15. How then can they hope to find the number of buttons required?

Further Explorations

1. How would you approach the buttons' problem with 5 year old children?

2. What problems could you follow up the buttons' problem with?

3. How soon would you expect children of this age to be able to master such problems?

◆ ◆ ◆ ◆

The teacher has all the children around her. She goes over the problem again to see if they understand what it is asking. Then she asks five of them, by name, to come out beside her. They each put on a large waistcoat. Each waistcoat has three buttons. The teacher gets the five "bears" to stand in a line facing the class. She then goes along the row and, with the help of all the class, she counts all the buttons.

"One, two, three, four, five, six, seven, eight, nine, ten, eleven, twelve, thirteen, fourteen, fifteen. We've solved the problem by **acting it out**."

The waistcoats are taken off. The five chosen children sit down. On her board, the teacher sticks up five drawings of the three buttoned waistcoats.

"Here's another way to find out how many green buttons the assistant at Arthur Barnett's needs. This time we're **using models**."

She then goes along the board and counts all the buttons with the children's help.

Further Explorations

4. List some other ways which can be used for solving the buttons' problem?

5. What skills is the teacher teaching the class?

◆ ◆ ◆ ◆

At this stage, the teacher might ask the class if they can think of any other way to do this problem. They may or may not be able to see that drawing the problem might help. She might even get some of the children to draw the bears and their waistcoats on the board. Again the teacher and the children count up to fifteen **using the drawings**.

But there is at least one other way that they could do the problem. There's bound to be some equipment in the room. The teacher takes 5 groups of 3 bottle tops. The bottle tops represent the buttons. This time, the count to fifteen **uses equipment**.

"How did we solve the problem?" she asks. "What was the problem? ... Does fifteen seem the right answer? ... What colour do the fifteen buttons have to be?"

The teacher may then say to the children that they have started to problem solve.

"We're going to look at a lot of problems like the buttons' problem this year. We're going to learn some strategies to solve these problems. We've already started. The strategies we used today were ..."

Further Explorations

6. Finish off the lesson for the teacher.

7. What similar problems would you do with these children?

8. What other problems might you do with these children?

    What strategies would these problems require?

◆ ◆ ◆ ◆

Now would be a chance for the teacher to give the children a problem for them to do in small groups.

"Before the bears go off to the picnic they have to put on their shoes. How many are there in Teddy's family?"

"Five."

"How many shoes will they need?"

"Before you go off and solve that, how will you do it? Will you act it out, model it, use equipment, draw it, what?"

After a little discussion the children go off to solve the problem.

Further Explorations

9.   What other problems could you make up about the Teddy Bears' Picnic?

10. What strategies do you think the children might try in the last exercise?

◆ ◆ ◆ ◆

"Would someone like to tell me how their group worked out how many shoes the teddies need?"

The teacher and class then discuss the problem. Not only is the teacher concerned about them getting the answer, she is also keen to see what strategies they use. In fact, she encourages them to use more than one strategy and she makes sure each strategy is used correctly.

"Which strategy did you think was best?"

...

"Why?"

Further Explorations

11. List the pros and cons of the strategies you have used in this section.

12. What do you think are the benefits of the last part of the 5 year olds' lesson - the reporting back stage?

2. WHAT IS PROBLEM SOLVING?

Before we answer that question we need to know what a problem is. A **problem** is a question or situation which, at the start, you have no idea how to solve.

Think about the teddies' buttons' problem. To you and me this was not a problem. We immediately knew that 5 times 3 was 15 and we were finished. However, for most 5 year olds this is a problem. Not having seen anything like this before, they will have to think of some way of tackling the problem. As we saw in the last section there are quite a few methods that can be used.

Let's make sure that we are clear on this then, a problem isn't a problem if you know immediately or instinctively how to solve it. The method of solution has to be discovered. Problem solving is clearly about solving problems. How we do this takes up much of this book. The point of learning problem solving here is so that we can teach it to our children. After all, problem solving is considered to be an important part of education and mathematics education in particular. **Problem solving** is something that today appears in the curricula of many countries.

Further Explorations

13. Write down some problems (They don't have to be mathematical ones, necessarily.) For whom are they problems? Is there anyone for whom they are not problems?

14. Is it possible that some children in this class see your problem as a problem and some don't? Would you only give a problem to your class if all of them saw it as a problem? Why?

15. What are the advantages of problem solving? What are the disadvantages of problem solving?

◆ ◆ ◆

There are a few other things that we need to get straight before we go too far here. One of these is a precise notion of three terms that will come up time and again in the rest of this book. First of all let's think about the word answer. By **answer** we'll mean an end result of a problem. In the problem in the last section, the answer was 15. You can have answers that are numbers, sets, "yes", "no" and almost anything else imaginable. It all depends on the way the problem is posed. The common thing that answers have, though, is that they finally settle the problem.

Then there are methods of solution. A **method of solution** is the way you got yourself from the initial problem to an answer. All the messing about we did in the last section, with acting it out, drawing and the like, along with a little counting, all these things together are the method of solution. Your method of solution for the buttons' problem is essentially multiplication. On more complicated problems, the method of solution will be more complicated.

Having done all the work, we get an answer. So we have solved the problem. By the solution of a problem we mean the combination of method plus answer.

solution = method + answer

So far, none of what we've said is peculiar to mathematical problem solving. In some ways it has nothing to do with mathematics even. If you have the problem of where to go for a holiday you'll choose a method for making the decision, you'll reach an answer, and so you'll have a solution.

The method will undoubtedly involve looking at your bank balance, thinking about where you might go, finding out which of your friends and family are able to go with you, and so on. Your answer to the problem will range from Paris, to going to Aunt Maud's, to staying at home. Put all that together and you'll have your solution.

Now when you tell someone your solution, you probably won't tell them all the gory details. You'll probably cut it down to "I'm going to Aunt Maud's because I can afford the bus fare, she won't expect me to pay too much for my board while I'm there and I enjoy the beach and her eldest son Tim".

Of course, it's exactly the same with maths. If we wanted to write up our solution to the buttons' problem, we might be able to do it in a single line. But if we did that, the reader would have no feeling for how difficult we had found the problem. They wouldn't have seen the dead ends that we met, or appreciated the number of ideas that we generated, or understood the choices we made along the way and why we made them. Our one line write up would probably make the solution look trivial. It would certainly say nothing about lining up five children and counting each of their three buttons.

And, when you think about it, that's what's wrong with mathematics. In maths textbooks they don't tell it like it really is. They don't show the reader how they came up with these fancy ideas. They present things, like Moses' tablets of stone, all complete and finished. No wonder when you read a maths book it all looks hard and inaccessible. If you could see it done step by step as it was constructed, you'd feel much happier about it. Of course, now and again someone had to have a brilliant idea or a bit of insight that most of us wouldn't have, even if we worked at a problem for a century or more. But a lot of it is just good hard slog and luck. People have ended up where they are by going down a million and one different paths and blind alleys. When they **did** get somewhere, they cut out all the fancy bits and reduced the whole thing down to size so it looked as if it came down from heaven in a black box tied up with a ribbon.

Further Explorations

16. Rewrite the buttons' problem so that the answer is 5.
    Rewrite the buttons' problem so that the answer is 3.

17. Write three problems for which the answer is "7 + 8 = 15".

18. Write two problems for which the answer is "a square".

19. Ask a colleague to produce a mathematical problem which has some answer that you have made up.

20. For the last few exercises, what is the method of solution and what is the solution?

The main difficulty with problem solving is coming up with a method of solution. If we have a correct method, then the answer usually follows fairly quickly. In some problems it turns out that it's relatively easy to **guess** what the answer is going to be. The hard part is justifying that guess, that is, finding the method of solution.

You may be surprised that we can have a pretty good idea of the **answer** to a problem before we know the **method** of solution. In the history of mathematics though, this has happened a lot. One case in point is the Four Colour Theorem. It turns out that for any map of the Earth (real or imagined), where two neighbouring countries are coloured differently, you don't need more than four colours. This problem arose in the last half of the nineteenth century when a student was colouring in the counties of England instead of doing his Geography homework. People quickly realised that they could colour all the maps they invented, with four or fewer colours. The guess that at most four colours were needed came very quickly. It wasn't until 1976 that the **method** of solution was found. Then we had the answer (four colours) and a solution.

So what do we do when we don't know how to solve a problem? One thing we try is **heuristics**. They're sort of strategies. The word means "serving to discover".

Heuristics don't necessarily go all the way to a solution but they put you on the right track. In the buttons' problem, for instance, acting it out is an heuristic that might put a 5 year old on the path to a solution.

Having a pocket full of heuristics is an advantage in solving any mathematical problem and that's one of the things this book is about. Of course, you can't solve too many mathematical problems without some mathematical skills. But this book won't provide too many of those. We expect you to have picked up most of the mathematics you need before you start in on the problems here. Though maybe from time to time you will need to ask someone how to perform a particular mathematical procedure in order to get a given problem out. As a teacher this gives valuable information about whether children know specific skills and how to apply them. If they do not know these skills, these problems may provide an appropriate opportunity to teach them. In this way there is a meaningful context for the children and this context often helps them to remember the skill better. We find that they often comment when using the skill later that they remember the problem they needed it for. For example "l ¥ w is the area of a rectangle. I learnt that doing the electric fence problem".

Further Explorations

21 What heuristics besides "acting it out" did we use on the buttons' problem.

22. Start an heuristics' file. Put each of the heuristics of this chapter on a separate page. Under the heuristic, put the problem that the heuristic was used in. Keep this file up to date with every new heuristic and every new problem you meet.

3. GEORGE PÓLYA

Pólya was a Hungarian mathematician who, in 1945, wrote an intriguing and innovative book called "How To Solve It". Among other things in that book he proposed a four phase method for solving problems. Every mathematical problem and maybe non-mathematical problem too, can be solved in the four phase way.

Pólya's four phases are

(i)   Understand the Problem
(ii)   Produce a Plan.
(iii)   Carry out the Plan.
(iv)   Look back over the solution.

The teacher in section 1 of this chapter followed that model. The first thing she did was to make sure the children understood the problem. To do this, it is sometimes useful to rewrite the problem in your own words. While you're doing this it's worth thinking about the key points of the questions. For our bears, the colours of the buttons were really unimportant. It was vital though that there were **five** bears and **three** buttons on each waistcoat.

We saw several plans to solve the problem depending on the heuristic. Basically the plans were to set up a situation so that with a bit of counting the answer would be obtained. Carrying out the plan gave the answer of 15.

At the end, the teacher listed all the methods of solution and compared them. Maybe there was one plan that was better than all the others. Maybe there was one plan that could be adapted for use with other future problems. Maybe there was a more efficient way of tackling the problem. Maybe different methods and answers will be appropriate for different levels of mathematical understanding. This often enables us to use the same problem with different ages and abilities but expecting different levels of sophistication in the solution.

Now in the buttons' problem the plan was to use a given heuristic, draw a diagram, say. Carrying out the plan this time gave the answer straight away. Things won't always be that easy. In more difficult problems, the first thing that you try won't always work. You'll need to back up and try another plan. So don't expect problem solving to be quite as straightforward as Pólya's four phase model might suggest. The importance of the model though, is that it gives some structure to problem solving and helps you to see that all problems have something in common. This should help you to solve them.

Future Explorations

23.   Read "How To Solve It".

24.   Lisa wrote down three prime numbers whose sum was 48. What were these prime numbers?

How many possible ways could Lisa have solved this problem?

25.   Use the last exercise to illustrate Pólya's four phase method of problem solving.

Pólya's four phase method can be summarised in the following poem.

Read the problem;
Heed the problem;
Choose a strategy;
Use a strategy;
Then look back.

In the first section of this chapter the teacher went through all of these steps. It's very important when solving a problem to understand what it says and what you have to find. A useful tip here is to underline the key points of the question.

Once you know what the problem **really** says, then you have to choose a strategy with which to attack the problem. Sometimes this is fairly straightforward. Many times a strategy suggests itself or, if you are lucky, many strategies spring forward. We'll worry about this as we go along.

After you've used the strategy you'll either have solved the problem or you will have got stuck. If you're banging your head against a wall, then go back to the question and start again. We'll have more to say on this as we go along.

But if you've solved the problem it is worth checking back to make sure you have indeed solved the problem. It's sometimes the case that you've overlooked an important aspect of the question and you may have to start again from scratch. If you have got the problem out though, it's worth thinking for a minute to see if you can come up with a neater solution. Then, of course, you can relax and listen to a CD.

Future Explorations

26. Write a story involving 9 and 23.

27. Write some problems having 13 as an answer.

28. Write a short biography of George Pólya.

29. List several ways of helping the children in your class learn to

(i)   understand a problem;
(ii)   produce a plan;
(iii)   carry out the plan;
(iv)   look back over the solution?

4. WHAT'S NEXT?

In the rest of the book we want to develop your problem solving skills and suggest some ways of teaching problem solving in your class. First, the skills. For a couple of chapters we'll go through some problems with you, so that you can see how we solve problems. During that time we'll list the strategies we use and you'll learn more about heuristics and other things. In between these chapters we'll do some reflecting on what is going on.

Then we'll use case studies. In these chapters we solve the problem on the left side of the page and provide a commentary on the right hand side. These comments are meant to underline ideas that have been introduced earlier.

The next chapter looks at mathematical patterns. Then, having introduced you to problem solving, and given you lots of practice at it, we return to the teaching of problem solving. These chapters outline the theory of teaching problem solving as we currently know it. We also emphasise that there is no one unique way to teach problem solving.

The book concludes with a chapter containing a number of lesson outlines for teaching problem solving. These are only illustrations of how some teachers approach the teaching of problem solving. They may be of some help to you as a guide when you adapt your own preferred teaching approach to include a problem solving dimension.

Future Explorations

30. Is it possible to accurately measure out 7 litres, given a 3 litre and an 8 litre jug?

    (There are no intermediate marks on these jugs. We only know how to measure 3 litres or 8 litres exactly, using a single jug.)

31. Suppose we have as many 3p and 8p stamps as we need. Is it possible to produce postage worth 7p using only 3p and 8p stamps?

32. Meg has twice as much money as Nick, and Nick has £20 less than Mary. Altogether they have £60. How much does each have?

33. Susan has 24 pets. Some are dogs and some are canaries. Altogether they have 54 legs. How many canaries does she have?

34. With her parents help, Donna had saved up £1 in 20p and 5p pieces. There were 14 coins in her savings. How many 5p pieces did she have?

35. George had 18 buildings blocks. He put them into 4 boxes so that each box contained a different number of blocks. How many blocks did he put in each box?

36. Seventeen of the 44 children in the class, wear glasses. Now 10 of the 21 boys in the class don't wear glasses. How many of the girls wear glasses?

37. Mrs Haddow's six children like white bread or brown bread or both. If four of them like white bread and five of them like brown bread, how many like both white bread and brown bread?

38. Merlin was training his young assistant in the ways of sorcery. "At the Round Table tonight, only Arthur, Bedivere, Kay, Lancelot and Morded will be seated," Merlin said.

    "Bedivere will sit to the left of the king, and Kay will sit to the right of Bedivere. Young Prince Morded will sit next to his father. If you can tell me where they are all to be seated, then I will yield to you the secret of magic fire."

    If you were Vivien, would you get to claim the secret of magic fire?

    (Sitting to the left of someone means that when they are passing the wine it gets more quickly to that person if it is passed to the left.)

39. Mr Bean has three ties, five shirts and two suits. How many days in a row can he go out and get into trouble wearing a different set of clothing?

40. Jane, Doris, Tessa and Colin all go for a swim in the sea. When they come back, they find that Doris' little brother Harry has put their T-shirts in a box.

    Now Doris' T-shirt matches her blue swimsuit. Tessa's T-shirt is her favourite colour and she doesn't like brown. Colin's T-shirt is not the colour that Tessa doesn't like. One person's T-shirt is green. Jane's mother bought her a new bright red hat. Tessa's favourite colour is the same as Jane's hat.

    Which coloured T-shirt belongs to which child?

41. Mr and Mrs Owen and their two children Tom and Trish want to row to an island. However, the boat will hold only one adult or at most two children. Can the Owen Family get themselves across to the island?

42. A magic square consists of nine smaller squares each containing a number, so that the sums of the numbers in each row, column and diagonal, is the same.

    An example of a magic square is shown below, where the sums are all 6.

3	1	2
1	2	3
2	3	1

    Can you find any other magic squares which use the numbers from 1, 2 or 3?

    Is it possible to find a magic square which uses each of the numbers 1, 2, 3, 4, 5, 6, 7, 8, 9?

    Is it possible to find as many magic squares as you want or is the number of magic squares limited in some way?

43. Freddo the Frog was trying to get out of a well. Every day he climbed up 3 metres but slipped back 1 metre at night. It was 11 metres from the water to the top of the well. How many days was it before Freddo got out of the well?

5. CHAPTER SUMMARY

In this chapter we introduced the following strategies:

> make a model;
> act it out;
> use equipment.

Some concepts are:

> a problem is a question which, initially, you have no idea how to solve;

> an answer is the end product of a problem;

> a method of solution is the way to get from the problem to the answer;

> a solution is the combination of method and answer:
>> solution = method + answer;

> an heuristic is a strategy that might help or does help to get all or part of a solution.

Pólya's four-phase problem solving model is

1. Understand the problem;
2. Produce a plan;
3. Carry out the plan;
4. Look back over the solution.

CHAPTER 2   THE PICTURES

1. THE PROBLEM

Let's move up the junior school a little and have a look at another lesson. The teacher, by way of introduction, asks: "Has anyone been to the pictures lately?"

The class discusses when they went to the movies and what they saw. They also talk about the fact that you have numbered tickets (and popcorn, etc, etc).

"Jo, Harry and Penny went to the pictures last weekend. When they were shown to their seats, they had to decide where they should sit. Who do you think sat next to whom?"

They then talk about the different ways they could be seated.

"How many different ways could Jo, Harry and Penny be seated?" the teacher asks.

They discuss this for a little while and the teacher encourages them to guess the answer.

"How will we find out exactly? What strategy could we use?"

The children may well come up with strategies that they have already learnt such as act it out, use equipment or draw a diagram. If the teacher has not had a problem solving lesson for a while she may well go through some of these strategies with the class.

The teacher notes the difficulty of acting it out. Clearly she can ask three children to take the parts of Jo, Harry and Penny. They can sit on three seats placed in a row at the front of the class. But there is a problem.

Further Explorations

1. Think about the three strategies for solving the pictures problem: act it out, use equipment or draw a diagram. Which of the strategies would you use? Why? What is the difficulty with acting it out?

2. Can you think of another strategy for solving the pictures problem? Is this better than the three methods mentioned above? Why?

3. Reword the problem using the names of children you know, possibly children from your class.

4. Make up a similar problem to the pictures problem.

◆ ◆ ◆ ◆

Although acting out the seating problem is fine, it's difficult to keep track of who has sat where. The same problem arises when you use equipment. The class begins to realise this. How could they **keep track**?

What about using a diagram? Well, perhaps not a diagram. Maybe a series of drawings though. The teacher starts to draw the three children on the board. You can see this in Figure 1.

Figure 1

At this stage, the teacher has two choices, she could continue with the drawings until all possible ways of arranging the three children have been exhausted or she could send the children off into groups to finish the problem for themselves.

If she has stayed at the board, she'll ask after each seating arrangement "Are there any more ways they could be seated?" If the children have worked in groups, she'll ask "Who can tell me how many ways they got? How do you know there are no more ways?"

After discussing the answers the teacher will point out the importance of being systematic. She might also say that this sort of problem can be done more quickly if we don't draw such good pictures of the three children each time.

Further Explorations

5. How could the children introduce a systematic approach into their drawings?

6. What could they do rather than use pictures for each child in the problem?

7. What would the teacher do if one of the children suggested another approach to this problem? What other approach might this be?

"What's the first letter in Jo's name?"

"J."

"What's the first letter in Harry 's name?"

"H."

"How about Penny's name?"

"P."

"It'll save us a lot of time if we use J for Jo, H for Harry and P for Penny instead of all those drawings. So if I write J H P that means that Jo sat in the first seat, Harry in the next seat and then Penny. What does J P H stand for?"

The children answer.

"Let's see what other ways there are of seating them."

The children suggest P J H, H J P and so on. The teacher writes them up on the board as they go until they have the list of Figure 2.

JHP
JPH
PJH
HJP
PHJ
HPJ

Figure 2

"Are there any more ways of seating the three friends?"

The children suggest "other ways" but they have all been put on the board already.

"How can we be sure that there aren't any more ways?"

"There just aren't!"

"How can we be certain though?"

The teacher then suggests that if they are **systematic** they can be absolutely sure that they have listed all the possible seatings.

Further Explorations

8. Write the seating list systematically so that it's clear that it exhausts all the possibilities.

9. What would you do next in this lesson? Why?

10. Can you solve the problem you invented in Exploration 4 by using a systematic list?

11. Suppose you had four children at the movies. How many ways can they be seated next to each other?

"Suppose we write the list again but this time we start with J for Jo. Who can we put next to J?"

"P."

"OK. So who do we put next to P for Penny?"

"H. He's the only one left."

"Right, so we start our list with J P H. If we start with J again can we put someone else other than Penny next to her?"

"Could put Harry."

"Fine, so that will give us J H P won't it? Can we start with J again?"

They discuss the possibilities and realise that J P H and J H P are the only ways to seat the three with J on the left end.

"Who else could be on the left end?"

" Harry."

"So let's start with him. Who could be next?"

"Jo", "Penny" are given simultaneously.

"Alright suppose we put J in the middle and P on the right. That will give us H J P. What other arrangement could we have with Harry first?"

"H P J."

"And are there any other arrangements with H on the left?"

The children realise that again there are only two seating arrangements with H first. These are H J P and H P J. They then realise that P should get her turn on the left. This leads to P J H and P H J.

"So we have the seating arrangements

$$
\begin{array}{l}
J\ P\ H \\
J\ H\ P \\
H\ J\ P \\
H\ P\ J \\
P\ J\ H \\
P\ H\ J.
\end{array}
$$

"Everybody has had their turn to be on the left. So there are no more ways to seat them. Altogether then there are six ways that the three friends can sit beside each other in the pictures."

Further Explorations

12. Is there an even **more** systematic way to list the six seating arrangements? Do you think that 6 year olds would be able to get to that stage?

13. How would you have solved this problem?

14. What important things do you think the children learned in this lesson?

    How could these things be reinforced?

◆ ◆ ◆ ◆

"Let's look at these arrangements."

The teacher points to Figure 3.

J P H
J H P
H J P
H P J
P J H
P H J

Figure 3

"It's a list isn't it? Like a shopping list. And it's systematic. We've carefully written the arrangements down in an ordered way. So we've got a **systematic list.** That's an important strategy that we will use in a lot of problems."

"What things do you notice about the list? Can you see any patterns? Paula, what have you noticed?"

"Each letter has two turns at being last."

"Sean."

"Each person has two turns at sitting in each position."

"Helen. What have you noticed?"

Further Explorations

15. Is a shopping list usually systematic?

Can you think of a list that you might make up which **is** systematic?

16. Can you solve Exploration 11 using a systematic list?

17. What would you do next with the class?

18. At the fast food chain Little Taffy's, you can get two sorts of drinks. Copsi and Peke, and three kinds of burgers, Small, Teeny Weeny and Minuscule. How many drink and burger combinations can you have consisting of one drink and one burger?

"I'd like you to think about this problem now. Tim has a red t-shirt and a blue t-shirt. He also has shorts and a pair of jeans. And he has a pair of sandals and a pair of trainers. He wears a different combination of shirt, pants and shoes each day of the week. How many days can he go before he has to wear the same combination again?"

"Now go off in your groups and get an answer."

Further Explorations

19. What answer did you get for Tim's clothing problem?

20. What method did you use to solve Tim's problem?

Is that the only way to do it?

21. Do you think the 7 year olds understood the problem before they went off in their groups? If you think "no", what extra would you have done with the class? If you think "yes", say why you think this way.

As they work in their groups the teacher checks that they understand the problem. She often does this by just listening to what the children are saying and observing what they are doing. Occasionally she'll ask a question to put them on the right track.

With some groups she might also ask what strategy they are using. She'll often ask why they are using that strategy even if it is a correct strategy.

Generally she tries to ask open questions rather than closed questions. So she'll say "Tell me what you are doing" rather that "Don't you think you should be doing this?"

When most groups seem to have got an answer, the teacher calls the whole class together and they discuss what they have done. Not surprisingly most children have made a systematic list. The teacher puts up a card on the problem solving board with "Try a systematic list" on it.

She then talks over the other strategies the children have used to see which worked. Anyone who didn't get the correct answer of eight has a chance to see where things went wrong. Both right and wrong answers are discussed. The bell rings for lunch.

Further Explorations

22. What do you think of that lesson? What were the good points? Which parts could have been improved?

    Give reasons for your comments.

23. What other cards do you think the teacher might have on the problem solving board?
    How will the teacher use these cards?

24. Some groups finish the problem, correctly, before the others. What would you expect these groups to do until the next instructions from the teacher?

25. Write another problem of the "systematic list" kind. Choose a topic for the problem that will be appealing to some children you know.

26. Toss three 10p coins simultaneously. How many possible outcomes are there?

27. Roll two dice.

    (a) How many different outcomes are there? (Here we are thinking that $6 + 1 \neq 3 + 4$.)
    (b) How many different totals are there?
    (c) How many times does each total appear?

28. Ying and Yang the Asian twins go to the pictures with Thelma and Louise. How many ways can they sit together so that the twins are always next to each other?

29. In the Olympic road cycle race, 52 cyclists start. Assuming they all finish, in how many different orders could they cross the line?

30. The de luxe restaurant the Upper Crust, serves entrées, mains and desserts. There are five entrées, ten main courses and six desserts. How many different meals is it possible to order given that each meal consists of one entrée, one main and one dessert.

31. Look back at Explorations 26 to 30. Which of these problems do you think can be done by children in which age groups, and why?

32. In Chapter 1 we suggested the following poem was a useful memory aid for problem solving.

Read the problem
Heed the problem
Choose a strategy
Use a strategy
Then look back.

Explain how the steps in this poem were used in the lesson of this section.

Was the poem any use in any of the exercises of this section?

33. Update your heuristics' file with the heuristics that you've seen used in this section.

2. ADVANTAGES AND DISADVANTAGES OF PROBLEM SOLVING

It seems appropriate to ask, about now, why people are interested in problem solving in general, and mathematical problem solving in particular.

Probably people have realised for a very long time that new situations crop up all the time in life. Many of these situations are similar to others we have experienced and so are not too difficult to deal with. On the other hand, some situations are completely new or we may not have quite handled them properly the last time. So being able to solve new problems is an important skill which our education system should be able to pass on.

But why mathematical problem solving? And why has it taken until relatively late in the day to decide that it is something that should be in mathematics curricula?

Before we tackle those questions we should point out that problem solving means more than just solving problems. It also means a problem solving **approach** to the teaching of maths. The point is that traditionally we, as teachers, have been fairly directive in our teaching of mathematics. In the past if we wanted to teach long division, we would set up an example on the blackboard, or more recently whiteboard or overhead projector, and showed our children how to do it. After one, or maybe two demonstrations, we would give them ten long division sums to do. We then went round and corrected their work, giving them a hand if it was needed. We'll refer to this method of teaching mathematics, as the **traditional** approach.

Most people were taught mathematics by the traditional method. It was the one approach which was to be commonly found at all levels from primary through secondary to tertiary levels. In this method, the teaching was of the variety that might be called the "sage on the stage" variety. The teacher was the expert who gave out knowledge to the children. On the other hand, the children were considered to be "tabula rasa", empty slates on which the teacher wrote information, or empty vessels into which the teacher poured knowledge.

As our understanding of the way children learn has developed, we have changed our attitude towards the teaching process. It is now believed that children construct their own knowledge based on their current understanding of the world. To fit in with this theory, we now feel that it is more appropriate for teachers to adopt the role of coaches, "the guide on the side", if you like. The teacher's role is to set up experiences for the children so that they can develop their own understanding of the things that society thinks are sufficiently important to put into school curricula.

By a problem solving approach in mathematics then, we mean the establishment of a classroom environment that promotes **investigation** of the subject, rather than rote learning. In such an environment, the teacher provides situations, generally based around problems, which will lead children to construct a meaningful and functional knowledge of mathematics.

Further Explorations

34. What has been the role of Piaget and Vygotsky in the development of our understanding of children's learning?

35. What is constructivism? How has it contributed to our theory of learning?

36. What does epistemology mean?

◆ ◆ ◆ ◆

The groundswell towards the problem solving approach to the teaching of mathematics began in the 1970s. Admittedly things had been happening before this. Pólya, for instance, wrote his important book, "How To Solve It", in 1945. But it was the 1970s which generated movements in Britain, North America, Australasia and elsewhere, which caused problem solving to become part of many national curricula by the mid 1990s.

Part of this drive was the realisation that mathematics has two faces. On the one hand there are the basic (and sometimes not so basic) **skills** that have been traditionally taught, and taught the traditional way. Such things as the four arithmetical operations, and their related algorithms, basic number facts, graphs and algebra are skills of this type.

On the other hand, mathematics has **processes**. These are ways of combining skills together, of working with known things to produce new things. They are the techniques by which research mathematicians produce new mathematics. Processes, however, have rarely been taught in the traditional mathematics classrooms. Clearly, experts in mathematics use these processes but, until recently, nobody thought it was worth teaching them in schools. Now it is recognised that mathematical processes are important for all students of mathematics, both to learn mathematics and to learn how mathematics is created. So with the development of the problem solving approach, came a major paradigm shift. This shift recognised that mathematics has not one by **two** main aspects. One of these is facts, skills and procedures, while the other, is processes. What's more both of these aspects is important. Certainly it is impossible to do problem solving without having access to basic skills.

Further Explorations

37. Find out about the Cockcroft Report. Why was it commissioned? What recommendations were made regarding problem solving and investigational approaches in the teaching of mathematics?

38. What is the National Council of Teachers of Mathematics? Why did it see fit to write An Agenda for Action, and Curriculum and Evaluation Standards for Mathematics? What were the main recommendations in these documents?

39. What is the Mathematics Curriculum and Teaching Project? What resources did it produce? What was its influence on problem solving?

Some of the advantages claimed for problem solving in schools are that it

(i)   bases children's mathematical development on their current knowledge;
(ii) is an interesting and enjoyable way to learn mathematics and engenders positive attitudes towards mathematics;
(iii) is a way to learn new mathematics with greater understanding;
(iv) is a useful way to practise mathematical skills;
(v)   encourages children to learn together in cooperative groups;
(vi) makes the child a junior research mathematician.

We don't intend to discuss these advantages now but we will come back to them later. We also, however, note that disadvantages have been claimed. Perhaps the two which stand out are that problem solving

(i)   takes up more time than the traditional method of teaching mathematics; and

(ii) is more difficult for teachers to teach.

Again, we will come back to these later.

Further Explorations

40. In the light of your knowledge of problem solving so far, comment on the advantages for the problem solving approach suggested above.

41. Can you think of advantages not on the list above? Why do you think they are important?

42. Comment on the disadvantages of problem solving above. Can you think of any other disadvantages? What are the difficulties that these cause?

3. CHAPTER SUMMARY

In this chapter we introduced the following strategies:

keeping track;
drawing a diagram;
being systematic;
making a systematic list.

The following advantages of problem solving were mentioned:

(i)   bases children's mathematical development on their current knowledge;
(ii)   is an interesting and enjoyable way to learn mathematics and engenders positive attitudes towards mathematics;
(iii) is a way to learn new mathematics with greater understanding;
(iv)   is a useful way to practise mathematical skills;
(v)   encourages children to learn together in cooperative groups;
(vi)   makes the child a junior research mathematician.

The following disadvantages of problem solving were discussed:

(i)   takes up more time than the traditional method of teaching mathematics; and
(ii) is more difficult for teachers to teach.

CHAPTER 3   A MOTHER'S DAY CARD

1.   BUYING A CARD

A class of eight year olds are having another problem solving lesson. The teacher, Ron has written a problem on a large piece of paper that he has hung by a paper clip from a small board and easel.

Sara and Matt have decided to buy their mother a card for Mothers' Day. Matt has put in 15p more than Sara. The card cost £1.25. How much did Sara pay towards the card?

Ron reads the problem over a couple of times to the children who are seated on the floor in front of him.

"How much did the card cost?" Ron asked the children.

"£1.25," one of them answered.

"What else is important?"

"It was a card for their mother."

"Would it be a different problem if they had bought a chocolate fish?"

"Their mother would have liked it better." The children giggle.

"But Tom, would it make any difference to how much Sara paid?"

"No. Only the numbers are needed for that."

"OK, so are there any more numbers in the question?" Ron asked the whole class.

"15 pence," Jane said. "Matt had 15 pence more than Sara".

"Right. How will that help?"

No one seemed to have any ideas about that.

"Fine, let's leave that for a moment." Ron had mentally ticked 'understand the problem' from his agenda for this lesson.

"What strategy would you use to solve this problem?" He knew the word 'heuristic' but felt that 'strategy' was a simpler word for them and it meant much the same thing. Lots of hands went up.

"Yes, Louise."

"Draw a diagram."

"How would you use a diagram?" Ron didn't have a clue how a diagram might help. It turned out that Louise didn't either. "Drawing a diagram is often a useful thing to do. If you see how to use a drawing here, let me know. Anything else?"

Using equipment, especially the play money that was kept in the corner of the room, was another suggestion made by a couple of children. A few other ideas were thrown into the ring. He reminded them of a problem that was a bit like this that they had done a few days ago.

"How did you do that problem?" he asked them.

Quick as a flash young Colin, one of the brightest children in the class said "in my noodle." Ron knew when he was beaten.

"Fine, now off you go in your groups. Use whichever strategy you can see how to use. I'll come round and see how you are going."

"I hate these problems," Fiona muttered to her friends as she went off to her group.

Further Explorations

1. What strategy do you think might work here? Try out that strategy and then find another one.

2. Can you see a way of using a diagram to solve the card problem?

3. Write (and solve) two problems that Colin might have been able to do in his noodle.

4. How would you have handled Colin's comment? Would you have pressed him further or not? Why?

◆ ◆ ◆

"We've done it." Mary's group beckoned to Ron as he walked past.

"Tell me what you did."

"Well, we got the long rods and called them 10 pence and the wee cubes we called 1 pence. Then we played around and found that 40 pence plus 85 pence was £1.25. So Sara spent 40 pence ..."

"... and Matt put in 85 pence," Terry added.

"Are you all happy with that?" They were. "OK. Just to make sure it's OK read the question again."

Mary read the question aloud.

"Do you see any problems with your answer?"

"We..ll. Matt has got 15 pence more than Sara ..."

"So is your answer correct?"

"Matt has 45 pence more than Sara."

"Perhaps you could have another try. Don't change your strategy though. That looks fine to me."

On going round to a few other groups Ron discovered that they had missed the fact that Sara had got 15 pence less than Matt.

Further Explorations

5. What would you do at this stage? Would you help each group individually to understand the problem? Perhaps you could call the whole class together and get them all to see that there was a key piece of information missing. But some groups seemed to be using that piece of information.

    Would you make a note to yourself to fix this difficulty next time you used this problem. Why? Why not? If you would, what would you do differently next time.

6. Would you have handled Mary's group differently from the way Ron did? Why? Why not?

◆ ◆ ◆ ◆

Ron stood on the edge of one group that was using rods to be one pence each. They had an awful lot of counting to do but they were guessing and checking. Better still they were checking both the £1.25 and the 15 pence. Actually, even better still in some ways, they had counted out precisely 125 rods and were splitting them up and counting the difference. It was slow progress, especially as they seemed to be changing their guess by only one or two rods each time.

Another group was using play money. Not surprisingly, they seemed to be working much more quickly than the rod group. In fact they finished as Ron came up to them.

"Well done," said Ron. "Now try the second question." He noted that after 15 or 20 minutes several groups seemed to have finished. There was about 10 more minutes until lunch, so he decided to have a quick reporting back session.

"Good. So how did you go? Can someone tell me what their group did?"

The one pence = one rod group told their strategy. They said they hadn't quite finished but they thought they were closing in on the solution using guess and check.

Colin said that his group had used the play money. They had guessed and checked too but they had realised that they could speed things up by changing by 5 pence amounts.

The one pence = one rod group were annoyed that they hadn't thought of that. "That's sort of cheating," one of them said grudgingly.

"Right," said Ron. "Louise did you manage to use a drawing?"

"We put down 125 little lines. Then we guessed the answer was somewhere in the middle. They put my pen between two lines. Then we counted all the lines on one side and all the lines on the other. We kept moving the pen to the left until the difference was 15."

"Well done. Did it take a long time?" It clearly had.

"What answers did you get?"

"Sara paid 55 pence," Fiona, who was not in the 125 little lines group, butted in at this point.

Ron was a little surprised at this because she wasn't the brightest child in the class.

"Does anybody agree with that?" he asked. Several of them had got that answer and had checked it. Ron was a little surprised that Fiona's group had got the answer in the time they had available. She wasn't in the top maths group, nor were the children she was working with.

Further Explorations

7. Fiona didn't use any of the methods we've talked about so far. Can you think of another strategy?

8. The large numbers involved here must have slowed the children down considerably. Would you make the numbers more manageable for children of this age next time or would you find a way around the problem?

Another group of children tackled the problem from the point of view of the difference rather than the sum. They argued that if they started with two amounts of money which differed by 15p, they could add the two amounts together. If the sum was £1.25, they were finished. If not, they could change the two amounts, still differing by 15p, until the total was £1.25. Having got to this stage, it was just a case of guess and improve. The more efficient children used a table like the one below (Table 1).

A	B	A - B	A + B	too high?
30	15	15	45p	low
60	45	15	£1.05	low
90	75	15	£1.65	high
80	65	15	£1.45	high
70	55	15	£1.25	√

Table 1

By adjusting A and B, while keeping A – B equal to 15, the children zeroed in on the correct answer.

Further Explorations

9. Repeat the problem assuming that Sara contributed 30p more than Matt and that the card cost £3.50.

10. Of all the methods used to solve this problem, which do you understand? Which do you think is the best? Why? Which would you encourage 8 year old children to use?

11. Write two problems which are of the same type as the card problem but which do not involve money.

Before Ron had a chance to ask Fiona how she had done the problem, Martin piped up "We got 55 pence too. Our group used Sharon's big sister's calculator."

"She said I could borrow it," Sharon said defensively.

"What a good idea," Ron said. "I'm sorry that I don't have enough calculators around for all of us to use. What did you do Martin?"

"We started with 20 and added 20 and 15. This was too low so we tried 50 and 50 and 15. This was still too low. Then we tried 60 + 60 + 15, which was too high. So we tried 55 + 55 + 15 and got 125!". Ron made a note to give them some lessons on calculators later.

"Fiona, what did your group do?"

"We used money too. But I said that we should push 15 pence away. Then I divided the rest of the money between Sara and Matt. That gave 55 pence each. So Sara had 55 pence."

Ron was surprised and delighted. What a neat way to do the problem.

Further Explorations

12. Did Fiona have a correct strategy? Is there a better strategy?

13. Those of you who know how to use algebra might do it that way.

14. Make a list of the heuristics that were used in this lesson and add them and the problem to your heuristics' file.

15. What heuristic did Fiona use? How could you classify it? Could it be used for any other problems than ones analogous to the Mothers' Day card problem?

16. How do you think the lesson went? What complications might arise if you tried this problem in a real class?

17. Did Ron incorporate Pólya's four phase problem solving model into his lesson?

2. LESSON FORMAT

In the first three chapters we have seen three lessons. We started with Teddy Bears and buttons, then we looked at a seating problem, and latterly we have considered Matt and Sara's Mothers' Day problem. They are not precise transcripts of actual lessons but they have been based very largely on actual lessons that we have observed. So we know that the kind of situation and responses we have written do actually occur in classrooms.

Further Explorations

18. What do the lesson formats have in common? Comment on the various aspects of the format of the lessons.

    What do you think is good or bad about them?

19. A lot of what was reported of the lessons was dialogue. In fact questioning was central to this dialogue. Can you see any common theme in the questioning? What are the strengths and weaknesses of the questioning?

20. What preparation do you think the teacher needed for each lesson?

    If you were the teacher, would have you bothered to try out any of the problems before you used them?

21. Did any of the children in any of the lessons come up with anything that you wouldn't have expected? If so, how do you think you would have coped with them?

◆ ◆ ◆ ◆

All three lessons that we have seen so far, consisted of three phases. These were

(i)   Beginning : Whole Class - Problem Discussion;
(ii) Middle : Group Work - Problem Solving;
(iii) End : Whole Class - Reporting Back.

In the initial stage of the lesson, the teacher spent time making sure that the children understood the question and its key points. Sometimes the teacher also talked about potential heuristics that the children might use. The whole of the beginning stage of the lesson was devoted to making sure that the children understood the problem and were able to get started when they moved to the next stage. This stage is a good time to recall problem solving strategies.

This initial period provides a good settling in time for the lesson as children change from another activity or come in from a break. The length of the first phase will vary depending on the age and ability of the children and how much you, the teacher, feel it is necessary to say and do. With older children you may decide it is sufficient to give them a problem written on a card and let them start by themselves. With weaker and/or younger children you'll probably feel it is necessary to spend longer ensuring that they have understood things.

Further Exploration

22. Give an example of a situation where you would make sure that the first phase of a problem solving lesson lasts (i) 1 minute; (ii) 5 minutes : (iii) much more than 5 minutes.

    What would you be hoping to achieve in each case?

In the middle phase of the lesson the children work at the problem in hand. This is generally done in groups, though you may decide that with a particular class, or for a change, you might want them to work on their own.

Children, especially young children, need practice in working together and working cooperatively. Hence you will need to spend some time at the beginning of the year ensuring that they learn cooperative skills.

Group size is another factor that you have to resolve. Experience seems to suggest that groups of size larger than four do not work well. This is mainly because of the physical set up and the kind of task being engaged in but it also has something to do with personalities.

Groups of size four usually are placed in two sets of two, facing each other (see Figure 1). Such groups can work well together if they engage in an activity to which they can all contribute. Suppose they are using building blocks to find how many towers four blocks high can be made with black and white blocks. Then the blocks can be placed in the middle of the table and each child can be involved in the problem. However, if they are working on a task which requires them to draw, they will either work individually or with A and B together and C and D together. In this kind of activity the physical situation causes the group to break into two pairs.

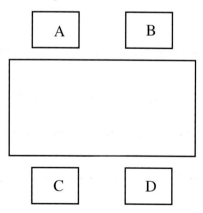

Figure 1

Similar problems arise with groups of three. If the activity is appropriately chosen, the children in such a group may work well together. But the physical arrangement may militate against the kind of activities which are common during problem solving.

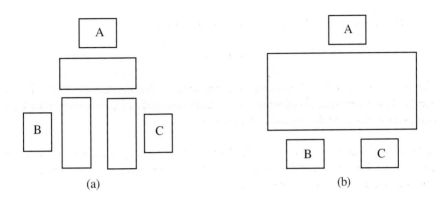

Figure 2

Groups of three children often are placed in one of the two arrangements of Figure 2. We have seen the set up of Figure 2 (a), where the right handedness of A caused that child to work with B, and C effectively became isolated. It is clear that in Figure 2 (b), A may be the one who is left out.

Hence with problem solving activities which require pen and paper, groups of size two seem to work best. Such groups can be encouraged to work even better together if they have only one piece of paper or one set of equipment between them. Of course, the big disadvantage of these small groups is that it takes the teacher a long time to get to see all the groups in action.

Further Explorations

23. Give problem solving activities in which the group shown in Figure 2(b) could function well.

24. Under what circumstances might child B in Figure 2(a) be isolated from A and C?

25. Are there other ways of arranging three and four children into groups that might work better?

26. How can groups of size larger than four be used profitably in problem solving lessons?

27. With groups of size two it takes the teacher a long time to see all groups. Is this problem insurmountable? Does the teacher need to see every group in every lesson?

The final phase of the lesson is the reporting back stage. The purpose of this session is not just to make sure that everyone got the right answer - the teacher probably knows this from going round the groups in the second phase anyway. Reporting back does give children a chance to communicate their solution. (We have seen children explaining what the last child said because they didn't think it had been explained too well.) Communication in mathematics has not generally been valued. However, we feel that by talking about their solutions, children begin to better understand what they have done. So communication is as important for the communicator as for the audience.

But reporting back time should be a thinking and learning time as well. It is likely that different groups will have used different methods to solve the problem. Reporting back gives all children a chance to share these methods and to store them up for use on a future occasion.

Perhaps surprisingly, we have seen reporting back sessions where the whole class has been totally silent and attentive while one of the children does the reporting. The child appears to have more control over the class than the teacher! We are not quite sure why this is the case. It certainly seems that all the other children are interested in what is being said. They are actively engaged in learning too.

Some teachers select a child at random to report back for their group. This pupil gives the report. Once it is given, other children from the group can add to the explanation. This forces each child to take ownership over what has gone on in their group.

Further Explorations

28. How long would you allow reporting back sessions to last? What would make you vary this time?

29. What would you expect the children in the class to gain from a reporting back session?

30. What other lesson formats are possible for problem solving sessions? In what ways are these better or worse than the three phase format given in this section?

The time frame for a problem solving lesson using the three phase format varies. Often it seems to take about forty minutes, though it can take much longer and spread over more than one session. In a high school setting, with a class of weak children, the lesson format was repeated at 10 to 15 minute intervals during the one period. With young children the smaller time frame may be an advantage too.

Finally here, we should note that the format of most lessons is not as simple as we have suggested here. Frequently the three stages are not covered in the order they have been listed. For various reasons it may be necessary to use the different parts a number of times in a lesson. Having said that it is worth noting that the three components we have isolated are valuable parts of a problem solving lessons.

Further Explorations

31. In what ways does the teaching of problem solving differ from the teaching of language?

32. When could you imagine the lesson format being Whole Class, Group, Whole Class, Group, Report Back?

33. Discuss other variations.

◆ ◆ ◆

3. TEACHER READINESS

What preparation is necessary by a teacher for a problem solving class? We'll try to give some answers to that question in this section but you may well want to think about it before reading on. Make a list of the things that you think are necessary.

The first thing that comes to mind is not that the teacher be an expert in mathematics with a degree majoring in mathematics. Teaching problem solving in the primary school will not require an advanced knowledge of algebra or familiarity with calculus or any of the other erudite subjects studied in higher mathematics.

Perhaps the two fundamental things that a teacher of problem solving needs is common sense and imagination. Much of mathematical problem solving, especially at the junior primary level, is common sense related to numbers and simple geometry. But teachers need to have the imagination to create an interesting environment for the problems, to see how to tie in the maths with their other subjects and to use the children's responses to their fullest.

Next on the list of qualities is openness and the readiness to take on a challenge. The teacher needs to be open to new ideas and to know how to ask open questions. It is important that the teacher not be afraid of new directions that children might find in a problem or be threatened if the conversation or the maths goes in a direction that had not been anticipated.

Then, and note that this is third on the list, the teacher must have had some problem solving experience. You have already looked at several problems in this book, so you've had some experience. You can begin to see how the process works and what you should look for when you get into difficulties. When you're first teaching problem solving you need to do the problems yourself first. That way you'll know at least one method and an answer. You'll also know whether it uses heuristics that the children can handle. If it's not a suitable problem you'll need to find another one.

Then there is imagination again, because you have to learn to think like the children in your class. What will they think about this problem? Will they enjoy the context? Do they have strategies to tackle it? What different ways will they do it? Will they have difficulties? What will these be? Will they be able to explain their methods? What methods will they have that I haven't thought about?

And when they do produce something unexpected you need to be able to handle the situation positively. This is what makes mathematics teaching fun, exciting and alive.

Further Explorations

In the following exercises we present a series of problems. We would like you to solve the problems using two or three different methods. Then decide the age of the children who would benefit by doing the problem. Reformulate the questions so that they would be suitable for those children. Finally, think where these children would get stuck and how you would help them out.

34. A worm sees 44 legs in a field. How many lambs are there?

35. Can you use a calculator to work backwards from 20 in twos? How many steps does it take to reach zero?

36. How many ways can you get 6 on the calculator? Can you organise your examples into an ordered list?

37. Eleven crocodiles swam down the river. Seven of them laid eggs. Those that laid eggs laid six eggs each. A greedy goanna ate fifteen eggs. How many eggs were left?

38. Peppi the Pizza Man delivered five pizzas to an apartment building. He delivered the first one to Mike Plummer on the sixth floor. It was a Petite Pineapple pizza, Then

he went up four floors to Marilyn Watson and gave her a Large Super Special. The lift went down seven floors and so he popped in to Honi Haki's and delivered a Quite Quaint Capsicum pizza. Peppi then took the lift up ten floors to the top floor, where Jane Austen received a Peppi's Pizza Platter. By this stage Peppi had forgotten who the last pizza was for and he ate it himself on the way to the ground floor.

How many floors were there in the apartment building?

◆ ◆ ◆

Oh, and there's one final thing. Perhaps the most important quality a problem solving teacher needs is patience. Our research suggests that you may see no significant change in children in their first 3 to 6 months of problem solving. However, once they build up a bank of heuristics, learn the cooperative skills necessary for group work, and experience the success and excitement of solving problems, you will be convinced that the changes are worth waiting for.

4. CHAPTER SUMMARY

In this chapter we used the following strategies:

using equipment;	making a table;
guess and check;	guess and improve.

One lesson format for problem solving has three phases:
(i)   Beginning: Whole Class – Problem Discussion;
(ii) Middle: Group Work – Problem Solving;
(iii) End: Whole Class – Reporting Back.

In group work we suggest you consider the group size carefully. You might like to work with pairs of children first and move up to larger groups, which are easier for you to service, as the childrens' group skills improve.

We suggest that to be ready to teach problem solving, a teacher needs:

to not necessarily have a degree in mathematics;
common sense;
imagination;
openness;
to be ready to take on a challenge;
to have some problem solving experience;
to solve the problem before giving it to the class;
to be able to handle the unexpected.

CHAPTER 4   THE TRUTH?

1. LADDERS

Let's get away from the classroom for a while and think of some problems for ourselves. Try this one.

There is a red, 2 metre long ladder, leaning against a wall. Well, actually it's standing right up against the wall. It's vertical. On a rung half way up the ladder is an ant. Her name's Frederica. The bottom of the ladder starts to slip. The ladder slides with the top always against the wall.

What path does Frederica move through?

Further Explorations

1.   Try to do this problem on your own. Don't forget to use Pólya's four-phase model
     - if it helps.

2.   What heuristics did you use in the ladder problem? How do you know you got the
     right answer?

◆ ◆ ◆ ◆

We're going to assume that you weren't able to solve the problem. We'll take you through the whole thing step by step. Compare your method to ours.

OK. So we first have to understand the problem. What's there to understand? Clearly it's important that the ladder stays up against the wall and slips slowly down. Though it could slip quickly down and it wouldn't change anything. So the speed is unimportant.

It's probably important that the ant is halfway up (down) the ladder. We're sorry to say though that it's not important that it's an ant and that her name is Frederica. And we can't see how the colour of the ladder could possibly affect things. But what about the length of the ladder? Hmm.

And what are we trying to find? "What is Frederica's path?" What does that mean? If she left dots behind her as she fell, what would the collection of dots look like by the time the ladder landed on the floor?

Further Explorations

3. Is the length of the ladder important? Why? Why not? Well, which and why?

4. Make a guess as to the shape the dots would form. This might give you an idea of what's going on. Check your curve of dots with someone else. Maybe take a vote on which curve is most likely correct.

How can you play around with this question? It's not as if we can put in some numbers and guess and check, or whatever. Ah, but what we can do is to draw up a wall and a floor and take a ruler and fit in various of the 'dots' we talked about. That way we might get a feel for what's going on.

But we could also imagine the ladder falling and try to 'see' what happens as poor Frederica falls. So let's do some mind experiments. A useful strategy is to look at some extreme cases. In this case, two extreme points on her fall are when the ladder first slips and when it stops slipping. Frederica obviously starts and ends in these places. So she could fall like this (see Figure 1), or this (Figure 2), or even this (Figure 3). We'd probably guess a smoothish path because it is obviously continuous.

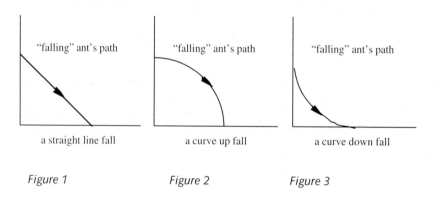

"falling" ant's path   "falling" ant's path   "falling" ant's path

a straight line fall   a curve up fall   a curve down fall

Figure 1   *Figure 2*   *Figure 3*

We somehow don't think that it's a straight line, like in Figure 1. Somehow that doesn't seem right.

The semi-circular looking shape of Figure 2 doesn't seem likely either. That's the sort of thing that you'd get if the foot of the ladder was stuck in the corner where the wall and floor meet. In that case, as the ladder fell, the top would mark out part of a circle. Not only that, but so would every other part of the ladder - including Frederica. So we suppose that that makes Figure 3 correct by default!

Further Explorations

5. Can you give a good reason why the path of Figure 1 is not right? The argument 'somehow that doesn't seem right' doesn't appear to be very convincing one way or the other.

6. Is it true that a ladder falling with its foot fixed in the corner traces out a bit of a circle?

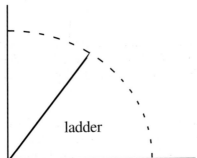

Does the dotted line in the diagram form part of a circle? Why?

7. If Fred (not Frederica) is halfway up the ladder in the diagram of the last Exploration, does he trace out part of a circle? What part of a circle?

8. Are you convinced that Frederica's frail body forms Figure 3? Why?

* * * *

Maybe we can settle things by drawing the situation. Get a stick (a ladder's really too big to handle unless there is a group of you) and find a suitable wall. Stick, or hold it on if you haven't got anything to stick it with, some chalk halfway up the stick. Let the stick slide along a wall and see what path the chalk traces out. We show the sort of thing we mean in Figure 4.

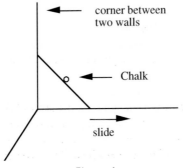

Figure 4

The difficulty with using this approach is that in holding the chalk and stick against the wall, it's difficult to get everything to slide down nicely. As a result you usually get a very shaky chalk mark. If you are a carpenter though, you'll probably be able to put together a fantastic working model that shows things very nicely. (Maybe you have a friend who is a carpenter?)

In the meantime, Figure 5 gives us another way of doing things. There we've drawn several positions of the ladder as it falls. The picture there makes it look pretty clear that Figure 3 is the sort of curve we're looking for.

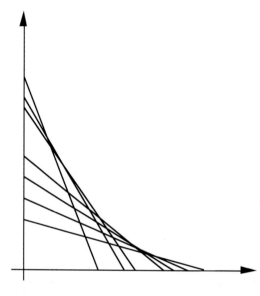

Figure 5

Further Explorations

9. After the experiments of Figures 4 and 5, what do you think happens to Frederica as the ladder falls?

10. By now you should have a pretty good idea of Frederica's falling. Write down a watertight argument to convince a friend that the way you say she falls, she actually does fall.

◆ ◆ ◆ ◆

Suppose we first guess that Frederica falls in a straight line. We could call this statement a **conjecture**. A **conjecture** is a statement which is testable. Here the conjecture is: Frederica falls in a straight line. Can we justify this conjecture or can we find something wrong with it? Remember the ladder is 2 metres long. This means, that Frederica starts 1 metre up the wall and ends up on the floor, 1 metre away from the wall. We mark these first and last points as M and N, respectively, in Figure 6.

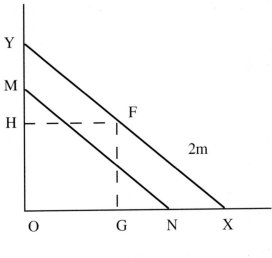

Figure 6

Where is Frederica when the ladder is half way down? In fact, where is the ladder when it's half way down? Presumably the top of the ladder is as far from the floor as the bottom is from the wall. In Figure 6, we show this by YX with Y at the top and X at the bottom. From what we just said, the distances OX and OY must be equal.

And where is Frederica? Halfway up the ladder. Half way between X and Y. You can see that in Figure 6 too.

Further Explorations

11. Given that the ladder is 2 metres long and that OX = OY, can you find the distances OX and OY? Use a scale drawing if you can't do it any other way.

    (Do you remember Pythagoras' Theorem?)

12. Whereabouts is F? Find the distances FG and FH, Frederica's height above the floor and distance from the wall, respectively.

13. What does the position of F, relative to the line MN, tell you? There are two useful things to note.

◆ ◆ ◆ ◆

According to the picture in Figure 6, Frederica is above the line between M and N when she's halfway through her fall. Where would she be if she fell in a straight line?

However she falls, Frederica starts at M and ends at N. In between we're not sure what happens. At the moment she could go on any of the three paths in Figure 7.

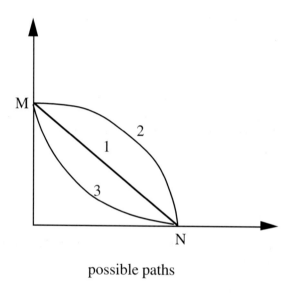

possible paths

Figure 7

But we're in business now. If, halfway down, she's at F, see Figure 6, then she's above the line MN. That means that at some point she's not on that line. So her path can't be the straight line graph of Figure 1. We've found a point F, that is completely at odds with the straight line guess. So the straight line is out; our conjecture has been tested and it failed the test.

At the same time Frederica can't fall down the Figure 3 path either. To do that, she would always have to be under the straight line MN and we know that F is above that line. So it looks as if its jolly old Figure 2. But is it part of a circle or just something with a bump in it that takes it away from MN? It would be nice if it was a circle. How can we find out?

Further Explorations

14. Draw another position of Frederica's ladder and very carefully find the midpoint.

    Use symmetry to find another point on Frederica's fall.

    Now find some more. Are all these midpoints on a circle. Why? Why not?

15. What property of circles do we need to use here?

    If Frederica's fall is a circle, what is its centre and what is its radius?

Have a look again at Figure 6. If you know about Pythagoras' Theorem you'll know that because XY = 2, and OX = OY, that OX = OY = $\sqrt{2}$. But then OF = 1. That's rather surprising because Frederica is a distance of 1 metre from O when she's at M and again when she's at N! We've got three places where she's a distance 1 from O. Is she always a distance 1 metre from O? If so, she's on the same circle as Fred in Exercise 7! Now that would be amazing!

Further Explorations

16. For the midpoints of the ladder that you produced in Exploration 14, was Frederica always 1 metre from O?

17. Is Frederica always 1 metre from O?

18. If Frederica's general position is x metres away from the wall and y metres above the ground, can you show that x2 + y2 = 1? (You'll need to use Pythagoras' Theorem and some similar triangles.)

    If x2 + y2 = 1, is Frederica always 1 metre from the wall?

19. Can you do this another way?

Forget about all the nonsense for a minute. Have a look at Figure 8. Frederica is at Q, halfway down the ladder. That shows four triangles inside a bigger triangle. What's more, there are a lot of right angles and AQ = QC.

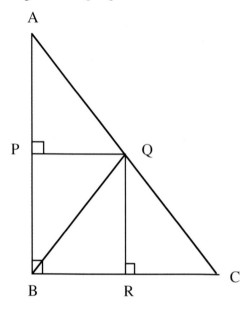

Figure 8

Because AQ = QC and PQ is parallel to BC, then AP = PB. But PB = QR, so that makes it easy to see that AP = QR. Similarly PQ = RC, which means that Δ's APQ and QRC are exactly the same, congruent if you like.

Surely though, this means that ΔQRB is the same as ΔQRC. So QB = QC.

If you relate that back to ladders, AQ = QC = 1. So QB = 1. So Q is always 1 metre from B. So Frederica is always 1 metre from B. So Frederica moves on a circle centre B and radius 1.

Go through this carefully and check that you understand each statement.

Further Explorations

20. (a) What heuristics were used here? Was there anything new?

(b) What heuristics would you have used if you had been doing the problem by yourself?

21. What help would you have given a person tackling this problem and when?

22. (a) Did this task need extra information not included in the problem?

(b) What mathematical skill would help you solve the problem more quickly?

(c) Make sure you understand the steps in the argument relating to Figure 8.

(d) Can you use coordinate geometry to solve the problem?

(e) Can you use the picture below to solve the problem? This shows Frederica's and Fred's ladders together. You know, they could actually hold hands as the ladders fall.

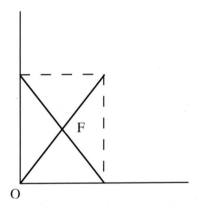

(Have you ever seen a folding chair fall in this way? The central points are joined and so must take the same path. Find a folding chair and try it.)

23. Often it is useful and interesting to think about whether the problem could be extended in any way. This is done by changing things a little.

(a) What would Frederica's path be if she was one third of the way down the ladder (from the top)?

(b) Investigate some other extensions of the ladder problem. (Vary Frederica's position or some other aspect of the problem.)

24. Reword the ant problem using a scenario that you think young children would find more appealing.

25. How could you use this problem with a class of primary school children?

2. JUSTIFICATION

The ant and the ladder problem of the last section illustrates an important aspect of problem solving and that is **justification**. Unless you can justify a solution you can't be 100% sure that it's correct. Unless you are able to satisfactorily explain what you have done and defend it against all challenges, you can't be sure that you have got it right.

There are three obvious contenders for the ant answer - straight, curved under, curved over. About the same number of people seem to believe that the answer is straight as believe it is curved over. Usually four times as many people again believe the curved under version (see Figure 3), is the correct one. Against those odds, how can you be sure that the Figure 3 answer isn't correct? If mathematical problems were decided by popular vote, Figure 3 would win hands down every time.

Justification varies with ability. What we would accept from young children we would not accept from their older sisters. But we would expect them all to be trying to justify their answers and their methods of solutions in a way which is appropriate to their level of development.

Of course, mathematicians use the word "proof" for their "justification". **Proof** is a cast iron argument that puts the matter beyond doubt. Mathematics differs from all other disciplines in that things can be proved in mathematics beyond any doubt. In law we accept **reasonable** doubt. The same applies in most sciences. However, if you are able to set up your logic and axioms properly in mathematics, certain things can be proved absolutely.

Proof is a powerful form of justification and producing proofs is a skill that takes time to learn. It is important that children learn to use a wide range of methods of justification in mathematics, starting at a young age. If the strengths and weaknesses of the various forms of justification are discussed from the start, children will gradually develop the idea of a proof.

Further Explorations

26. How did we justify the Teddy Bears' button's problem? Did we actually provide a proof?

27. How did we justify the Picture seating problem? Did we actually provide a proof?

28. How did we justify the Mother's Day card problem? Did we actually provide a proof?

29. What is the difference between a justification and a proof?

◆ ◆ ◆ ◆

Proof is a special kind of justification. But proofs don't have to be sophisticated things that only geniuses can aspire too. Take the Pictures problem from Chapter 2, for example. You remember we wanted to know how many ways three children could sit in three adjacent seats at the pictures. We did this by making a systematic list and verifying that there were precisely six possibilities.

Making a systematic list which exhausts all options is a perfectly good **proof**. It demonstrates beyond any doubt what the answer is. What's more it can't be challenged. If someone should say "Well, you didn't cover such and such an arrangement" you would be able to correctly say "Yes I did". You can also be sure that there are no more options to be covered.

Note that the emphasis here is on **systematic** list. A list of all six possibilities in some **random** order does not constitute a proof. You can, of course, counter the argument "Well, you didn't cover such and such an arrangement". All you do is just look down your list and show that such and such is there. But you can't be sure that you've covered **all** arrangements. Unless you do things systematically, you can't be sure that there's a seating arrangement that you haven't missed. So a non-systematic list is only a partial proof that there are six seating arrangements. A random list does give some justification that the answer is six but there is always a little nagging doubt.

Proofs are watertight justifications where the little gaps in the argument are closed up. It is important to ask yourself "Is there any way that I could make my justification and explanation more thorough?", that is, more like a proof.

Further Explorations

30. Will the guess and check heuristic give a proof or only a justification?

31. In the Picture seating problem we could give the following justification.

    "The first seat can be filled in three ways, then the second in two ways and the third in only one way. Now $3 \times 2 \times 1 = 6$. So there are six ways of seating the kids."

    What do you think needs to be added to that to make it a proof?

32. Give a proof of the fact that Frederica falls through a quarter of the circle whose centre is at O and whose radius is 1 metre.

3. CHAPTER SUMMARY

In this chapter we used the following strategies:

> try extreme cases;
>
> using equipment (chalk and ruler);
>
> acting it out (well Frederica actually did);
>
> using drawing.

We introduced the ideas of:

> conjecture (a guess that is testable);
>
> extension (a new problem obtained by varying an old one);
>
> justification (a means of making sure your solution is correct);
>
> proof (a watertight justification).

CHAPTER 5 SUBTRACTION

1. ANOTHER PROBLEM!

Try this one on for size.

There are two subtraction problems below. They both have the same answers. The letters a and b stand for the same digits in each problem. What numbers do a and b represent?

400	4ab
- ab4	- 400

Further Exploration

1. See what you can do with that problem. We sometimes find that the usually very top children in the class don't do it as quickly as some of the others.

◆ ◆ ◆ ◆

The reason that quite clever kids have trouble with this one is that they try to use algebra. Now algebra will work but it's best to hold algebra in reserve until it's really needed. How far can you get by just **thinking** about the problem?

We are always surprised when someone says a = 3 and b = 6. Though they may well say b = 6 and then say a = 3.

Further Explorations

2. Did you get a = 3, b = 6? How?

3. In your answer to the "How?" part of the last Exploration, did you manage to provide a full justification (a proof)?

4. Are there any other answers besides a = 3, b = 6?

◆ ◆ ◆ ◆

Now that we've taken the unusual step of giving you the answer, it's easy enough to check it. Just substitute 3 and 6 for a and b. We'll do that now.

$$\begin{array}{r} 400 \\ -364 \\ \hline 36 \end{array} \qquad \begin{array}{r} 436 \\ -400 \\ \hline 36 \end{array}$$

The answer is 36 in both cases so we must have had the right answer.

Further Explorations

5. How do you get the right answer in the first place?

6. How do you know that there is only one answer?

We suggested that you didn't use algebra but you could. If you did you'd be faced with something like

$$400 - ab4 \qquad = \qquad 4\,ab - 400$$
$$400 - (\,a \times 100 + b \times 10 + 4) = 4 \times 100 + a \times 10 + b - 400.$$

Rearranging (we'll let you sort out the details) gives

$$36 = a \times 10 + b.$$

Clearly $a = 3$ and $b = 6$ is the only solution.

But it's much quicker to notice that in the original subtraction sums, the digit in the units column of the answer in the left sum is 6 and so the corresponding digit in the right sum is 6. So b has to be 6. So then we have

$$\begin{array}{r} 400 \\ -a64 \\ \hline ..6 \end{array} \qquad \begin{array}{r} 4a6 \\ -400 \\ \hline ..6 \end{array}$$

Now looking at the ten's column we get 3 on the left and a on the right. So $a = 3$ and we're finished.

Further Explorations

7. How many justifications have we given for the 400 problem?

How many proofs have we given?

How many of the justifications can be made into proofs?

8. Can you find another proof?

2. EXTENSION

Very often when you have a problem like this you can make up another similar problem. For instance, why were we so concerned with 4? Why not replace all of the 4s with 5s? That gives us the following problem.

For what values of a and b do the two subtraction sums below give the same answer?

$$
\begin{array}{r} 500 \\ - \underline{ab5} \\ \ldots \end{array}
\qquad
\begin{array}{r} 5ab \\ - \underline{500} \\ \ldots \end{array}
$$

Further Explorations

9. Find a and b in the sums above. Prove that your answers are correct.

10. Can you use the same method of solution on the 5 version of the problem as you did with the 4 version?

◆ ◆ ◆

What we've done here, going from the 400 version of the problem to the 500 version, is called **extending the problem**. An **extension** of a problem is a problem which is similar to the first in some respect. Here the format of the two problems is the same. The basic idea is the same. We've only changed the digit "4" to the digit "5" every time it occurred.

You've actually been the victim of the extension game already. When we were looking at the cinema problem in Chapter 2, we gave you an extension of that problem. The original problem had three children involved. Later on, in Exploration 11, we replaced "three" by "four". The problem with four children is an extension of the one with three. Obviously you could extend the problem to five or six or six hundred children if you wanted to. The only limitations are time, motivation and imagination.

Further Explorations

11. Find two extensions of the Teddy Bear's buttons' problem.

12. Find two extensions of the Mothers' Day card problem.

13. Find two further extensions of the 400 problem. Make sure one of them, at least, is quite a different extension.

It may not have occurred to you that we can change the number of digits in a problem as well as the digit itself. An interesting extension of the 400 problem is the 4000 problem. We get there by looking at the following two subtraction problems. What values of a, b, c make their answers equal?

$$\begin{array}{r} 4000 \\ -\ abc4 \\ \hline \cdots \cdots \end{array} \qquad \begin{array}{r} 4abc \\ -\ 4000 \\ \hline \cdots \cdots \end{array}$$

By now we know how to do this. The unit's column on the left is 6 so c = 6. Then the ten's column on the left is 3 so b = 3. Then the hundred's column on the left is 6 so a = 6. And that just about wraps that up.

Further Explorations

14. Solve the two 400 extension problems that you posed in Exploration 13.

15. Give a proof that a = 6, b = 3, c = 6 in the 4000 problem.

3. GENERALIZATIONS

There's nothing to stop us extending ourselves for quite some time on the 400 problem. We could look at the 100 extension, the 200 extension, the 300 extension, and so on up to the 900 extension. We'll stop there just for now because we can see a **generalization**. The generalization of the 400 problem we've seen is the following.

Suppose x = 1, 2, 3, 4, 5, 6, 7, 8, 9. Then find a and b if the following two subtraction sums are equal

$$\begin{array}{r} x00 \\ -\ abx \\ \hline \cdots \cdots \end{array} \qquad \begin{array}{r} xab \\ -\ x00 \\ \hline \cdots \cdots \end{array}$$

This problem is a **generalization** of the 400 problem in that it contains the 400 problem as a **special** case. Putting x = 4 gives the 400 problem. But putting x = 5 gives the 500 problem and so on. So the x00 problem includes nine problems, one of which is the 400 problem.

Further Explorations

16. Give a generalization for the Teddy Bears' buttons' problem.

17. Give a generalization for the Picture seating problem.

18. Give a generalization for the Mothers' Day card problem.

19. Solve the x00 problem. A solution here will mean values of a and b that depend on x. The dependence will be such that when x = 4 you'll get a = 3, b = 6 and when x = 5, then a = 4 and b = 5.

(You don't need algebra to do this.)

A horrible thought has come to us. One of the extensions of the 400 problem didn't get a thorough overhaul. We missed checking the thousands column.

The reason that this has been bugging us is that it doesn't seem right to have a = 6! Think about it now. We had the two equal subtraction sums

$$
\begin{array}{cccc}
4000 & \text{and} & 4abc \\
-\ abc4 & & -\ 4000 \\
\cdots & & \cdots
\end{array}
$$

We said that a = 6, b = 3, c = 6. But if a = 6, the subtraction sum on the left gives a **negative** answer, while the one on the right is **positive**.

We've come across a problem here that **can't** be solved. It has no answer. Have you ever met a problem with no answer before?

Further Explorations

20. Does the 5000 problem have an answer? In other words do there exist digits a, b, c so that the two subtraction sums below are equal?

$$
\begin{array}{ccc}
5000 & & 5abc \\
-\ abc5 & & -\ 5000 \\
\cdots & & \cdots
\end{array}
$$

21. Generalise the 4000 problem. What is the answer to that generalization?

22. Extend the 400 problem again.

Generalise the extension.

◆ ◆ ◆ ◆

We've already solved the x00 problem, the generalization of the 400 problem, for two values of x, namely x = 4 and x = 5. So we could make up a table and work out the values of a and b for all values of x. We've started that in Table 1 below.

x	a	b
1		
2		
3		
4	3	6
5	4	5
6		
7		
8		
9		

Solution of the x00 problem

Table 1

Now that we've got the hang of these problems, it shouldn't be too difficult to work out a and b for all x. The method is just the same as the method for x = 4.

Further Explorations

23. Complete Table 1.

24. Given the result of Table 1, can you find a way of getting a and b given the value of x. (You don't want to have to remember the table !)

25. State and solve the x000 problem.

◆ ◆ ◆ ◆

The track we are going down is really an **investigation**. That is sort of "open" problem solving. You see problem solving, as we said earlier, involves us working with one closed problem. Naturally we'll need to use heuristics and all that but when we've solved the problem, we've solved the problem. What's more we know when we've solved it. But investigations are up to us. Usually there's no well-defined problem. We just take it where it seems to want to go.

With this 400 problem we had just a simple problem. But then we suddenly saw how to extend it and generalize it. What we ended up doing was beginning an investigation into the 400 problem and any or all extensions and generalizations. So far this extension has involved us with the x00 problem the x000 problem and even the x0000 problem. Where will it all end? That's the problem with investigations. They go on until we get tired, run out of motivation or don't have the wit to think of a new extension or generalization. In some sense, mathematics is one wild investigation - a problem that we keep making up, generalizing and extending as we go.

Further Explorations

26. Base an investigation around the Pictures seating problem.

27. Can you base an investigation around the Mothers' Day card problem?

28. How many ways can a square be cut in half? Investigate.

29. How many different shapes can you make with three sides?

30. Investigate adding 8 to numbers ending in 5.

31. Are the tallest people the heaviest?   Are girls heavier than boys?

4. A MODEL OF PROBLEM SOLVING

We've now done enough problem solving so that we can stand back and have a good look at what we've done. There seem to be some distinct stages in problem solving. First we'll look at Pólya's four phase model again and then we'll look at an experimental model of problem solving which cuts across Pólya's model.

If you recall, from Chapter 1, Pólya's four-phase model is
      (i)   Understand the problem:
      (ii)   Devise a plan;
      (iii)   Carry out the plan;
      (iv)   Look back over your work.

The four steps of this model certainly all exist and contribute to solutions of the problem. One thing that is worth noting though, now that we have solved a number of problems, is that problem solving is not as linear as the model suggests. The four phases do not always follow precisely in the order given.

For instance, it may be that the first heuristic you try, when you devise a plan, doesn't work out. When you carry out the plan you are not able to carry it to completion. Now this may be because you have not understood some part of the problem. You may have missed a key piece of data. So you will have to go **back** from phase ii to phase i.

These little hiccups occur all the time in problem solving. It is unlikely, unless the problem is easy or you are very lucky, that you will go straight through the phases in order, i, ii, iii, iv.

Another model is based upon the experimental sciences model. We show the main stages in this below.

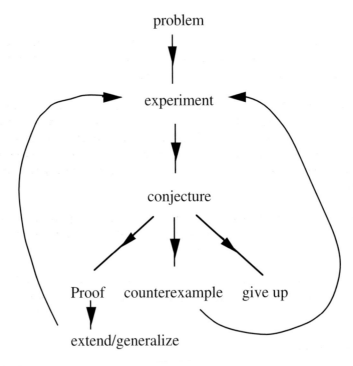

Given the problem we first experiment to get an understanding of the problem and a feeling for the solution. This leads to a **conjecture**. This is a guess of what the solution may be. In the last chapter, you may remember with the ant and ladder problem we initially had three possible conjectures for Frederica's falling path.

At the conjecture stage we may have to **give up**. There is no guarantee that we will always be successful. But sometimes 'giving up' is a good problem solving strategy. For some reason we don't really understand, after we've spent some time working on a problem, even though we have given up, our brain hasn't. Somewhere in the depths of the brain, some cells seem to keep working on the problem. If we're lucky, these cells will get a good idea and send it up to where we can use it. Have you ever had sudden bright idea in the shower or walking the dog? Giving up then, can sometimes lead to a solution. Unfortunately you can't rely on it.

If we are lucky though we may find a justification that can be made into a proof. On the other hand, if the conjecture is false then we might be able to find a **counterexample**. This is some example which shows us that our conjecture is false. The fact that we were able to find a point on Frederica's path which was **above** the straight line we had conjectured, gave a counterexample to that conjectured path. The trouble with finding a counterexample is that another conjecture has to be found and we may have to go back to experimenting again.

In the case of finding a proof we may sit back and rub our hands with glee, thankful that we have solved the problem. Alternatively, we may find an extension or a generalization of the problem and the whole business starts all over again.

Of course, although this model pretends to be less linear than Pólya's model, it is in fact even less linear than it pretends. One particular tension that we have not mentioned is that between proof and counterexample. Looking for a counterexample often provides evidence for a proof and vice versa. We saw this in the ant problem. The existence of a point above the straight line dealt a blow to two counterexamples but led to the justification of the quarter circle shape.

But in the experimental model there should be arrows all over the place. Just as we said in Pólya's model, you may at any time need to go back to the problem to find data that had previously been overlooked. Or an experiment may suddenly lead to a proof, and so on.

Problem solving then, is too complicated to model exactly. However, models do give us some idea of the key points and how they link. As such they sometimes help us to solve problems.

Further Explorations

32. Compare Pólya's model of problem solving and the experimental method. What do they have in common? How are they different?
33. Analyse these models with respect to problems you have solved so far. Which is the more effective model? Why?

34. Design your own model of problem solving. What aspects would you include in your model which aren't either in the Pólya model or the experimental model?

35. Generalize the Mother's Day Card Problem from Chapter 3.

36. Bring your heuristics' file up to date.

5. CHAPTER SUMMARY

In this chapter we used the following strategies:

> make a table;
> by systematic.

We also introduced a scientific problem solving model. This proceeded from the problem to a conjecture via experimentation. The conjecture then has to be settled, a counterexample found or we have to give up. If we can find a proof we might move on to a generalization or an extension. In this context, a generalization is a broader problem which contains the initial problem as a special case.

An investigation is an open problem solving situation where we follow generalizations and extensions until we run out of ideas or time.

CHAPTER 6 WHAT'S IT ALL ABOUT?

1. THE TEMPLE OF GLOOM

Somewhere, in a steamy part of planet Earth which is infected with mosquitoes, snakes, poisonous spiders and all manner of other nasty creatures, Indy Anna-Jones has got herself trapped in another Temple of Gloom. In order to activate the delicately balanced combinations of granitic rock blocks that will shoot her to the surface and to safety, she has to put the 21 stones in the six circles in front of her. Those circles are placed to make an equilateral triangle, each circle has to get at least one stone. But there has to be a different number of stones in each circle and the sum total of the number of stones in each side of the triangle has to be the same.

Indy Anna-Jones naturally realised in a flash what she had to do as she translated the ancient inscription, surrounded by skulls and other fear provoking images, carved on the wall before her. Naturally, failure to solve this conundrum from times past would mean a lingering hell below ground because she was running low on her supplies of Chanel No. 6.

Of course, this all boils down to, can the numbers 1, 2, 3, 4, 5, 6 be placed in the circles in Figure 1, one number to each circle, so that the sum of the numbers on each side of the triangle are equal? But Anna-Jones didn't need to translate this into English as the ancient inscription was in one of the 734 languages in which she was fluent.

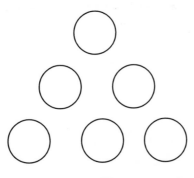

Figure 1

Some of you may have seen this problem before. It's fame has somehow escaped from the underground cavern. The first time we saw it, it was being presented at an EQUALS workshop. Our immediate reaction was panic. This was like nothing else we had seen before. How on earth could it be done? You have no need to panic. Indy Anna-Jones didn't panic. There is no Temple of Gloom fate awaiting you and no workshop leader standing beside you waiting for you to get going. Get a piece of paper and see what you can do with the problem though.

Further Explorations

1. Can you find a solution to Indy Anna-Jones' problem?

2. Is there only one solution to this problem?

3. What heuristics did you use to solve this problem?

Just run through the problem again. Six circles, six numbers. One number in each circle. All three numbers on each side add up to the same thing. As the old Jedi master once said, "Possible is it that can happen this?"

Now there are only six digits that we can use. If the worst comes to the worst, then tossing in a few numbers here and there will probably get us the answer. ... Hmm. ... The worst has come. Let's do a bit of trial and error.

What if we try putting the 6 in a corner? (After all it has to go somewhere and if you think about it, by symmetry there are only corner circles and side circles. There's really not much choice then.) Since we are trying to get equal sums on each side of the triangle, it might be a good idea to spread the bigger numbers out as far as possible. Perhaps then, the 5 and 4 should go in the other corners? Ah, yes. We can now finish things off by balancing up the sides with 1, 2 and 3 to give the answer in Figure 2. So we can put the numbers 1, 2, 3, 4, 5, 6 in the circles in Figure 1, so that the sum of the numbers on each side of the triangle are equal! Indy escapes again!

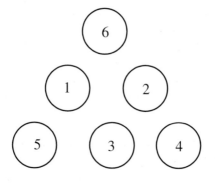

Figure 2

Further Explorations

4. Did you find the solution given in Figure 2? If not, did you check that that solution works?

5. How many solutions have you got now?

6. Do we really have symmetry in this problem? Surely it matters whether 6 rocks are put in the top corner circle or one of the circles on the corner at the side?

◆ ◆ ◆ ◆

When you think about it, that wasn't so much trial and error as wildcatting. We plain guessed what was going on and hoped that we hit on an answer. We didn't really trial anything and then discard it if we found it wasn't right. Well, maybe not much anyway. The problem was relatively easy or we were lucky. Anyhow we essentially wildcatted the answer.

So we've answered the problem. Indy Anna-Jones answered it too, the same way. Did she immediately put 6 stones in the top circle, then 1 and 2, and then 5, 3 and 4? Or did she stop a moment and reflect? She actually recalled the time that a similar hasty decision set loose a large spherical boulder which chased her down a narrow passage way. She waited a moment and asked herself the natural question "what would a mathematician do?". Ah, yes ... Then she phoned up Professor Themes the well known mathematician on her cellphone. He solved the problem in 10 seconds.

This is a book about mathematics. At this stage then, it might be worth asking what a mathematician would do next. Now you may never have seen a happy mathematician because they always have problems. And the reason they always have problems is that (a) members of the public keep asking them silly questions about rocks in circles and (b) they can see problems where the rest of us can't. In the problem of the six circles, a mathematician would ask "Is there more to find out?" For instance, is there only one answer to this problem or are there a whole lot more that we haven't found yet? **Can** we find all the answers? **Have** we found all the answers? Does our answer satisfy all the conditions of the Temple of Gloom problem?

Actually a bit more wildcatting will get us another three answers. They're shown in Figure 3. Did you manage to find any more?

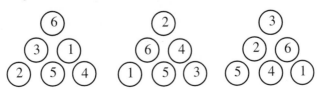

Figure 3

Of course you might have found these answers but you haven't realised it. If you think about it a bit, you'll see that you can rotate the triangles in the Figures 2 and 3 and flip them about axes of symmetry, to get what look like different answers. When you think about it more though, none of these is essentially different to any of the answers we get from Figures 2 and 3 combined.

Further Explorations

7. Can you convince yourself that there are essentially only four answers to the Jones' problem?

8. Perhaps the working conjecture here is that there are just those four answers. Can you justify, or better prove, this conjecture?

◆ ◆ ◆ ◆

Well, we don't know how much time you have put into it but we can't find any more answers. How can we be sure there aren't any more though? (This is the mathematician talking again. Most of the rest of us would be happy to stop at this point and have a cup of tea or even something a bit stronger.) How could we be sure of finding the rest, if there were any? Which is the right way of putting the stones in the Temple of Gloom? Will they all do?

One certain way to check we've got all the answers is to do a **systematic search**. That way we'll flush out all possible answers. To go down this route there seem to be a lot of possibilities to try though. There are six possible circles that we can put the 6 in. There are then five possible circles left to put the 5 in. After that there are four circles that can take the 4. Then there are three circles that could play host to the lovely number 3, followed by two circles still left for the 2 and then we've only got one circle left to put in the 1. This gives a total of $6 \times 5 \times 4 \times 3 \times 2 \times 1 = 720$. If we do a systematic search there are 720 ways of filling the circles. Each one of these 720 ways then has to be tested for the "equal side sum" property. That might be OK for a computer (maybe you can get going on with the programming as we speak) but it looks an unnecessarily long task by hand. It seems that it really is drinking time now.

Further Explorations

9. Check the argument that led to 720 possibilities. Doesn't symmetry count for anything here? Surely symmetry ought to reduce the number of trials by quite a lot?

10. Devise a systematic search for this problem.

◆ ◆ ◆ ◆

But hang on. We don't have to put all the numbers into all the circles and check all 720 possibilities. We can cut the possibilities down by using the symmetry of the equilateral triangle that we talked about before. So let's see where the 6 can go. We have already said that any number is either in a corner circle or a side circle. So there are really only two places to put the 6 after all. And a little rotation or reflection will get the corner circle to the top. Suppose we try the 6 in the top corner circle. That'll be Case 1. (By the way, this may get a bit heavy on the first run through. Get a feel for what's going on and then come back to it again later.)

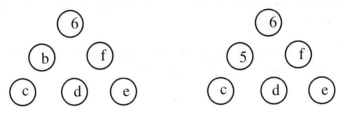

Figure 4

Now there are three places the 5 can go: in circle b (but that's the same as f by symmetry), in circle c (the same as e), or in circle d. So those choices for 6 and those for 5 reduce the number of possibilities to 2 x 3 x 4 x 3 x 2 x 1 = 144. That's a big saving on 720. And the Chanel No. 6 is running down.

Now we'll break Case 1 into three subcases.

Case 1.1 Put 5 in b (see Figure 4). This clearly is a problem. First of all, none of the four answers we've found so far has 5 next to 6 like this, so we're probably in trouble here. Worse still 6 + 5 = 11 which is greater than 1 + 2 + 3 + 4. There's no way we can put any of the remaining digits in c, d and e so that the side containing 5 has the same sum as the c, d, e side. So 5 can't be in b.

Case 1.2 Put 5 in c (see Figure 5). We already know that we get one answer this way. So let's see if that's the only one. With 6 and 5 on the left side, that side's sum is at least 12.

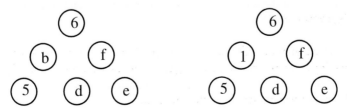

Figure 5

Note now that the biggest $5 + d + e$ can be is $5 + 4 + 3 = 12$. So b can't be any bigger than 1. Our only hope is that b is 1. If it is, then this forces d and e to be 3 and 4. But if $e = 3$, then f needs to be 3 to get the $6 + f + e$ side up to 12. So d has to be 3. This forces e to be 4 and f to be 2. Seen that somewhere before! Our systematic search has come up with its first success.

Case 1.3 Put 5 in d (see Figure 6). We know from Figure 3 that there's at least one solution coming up but are there more?

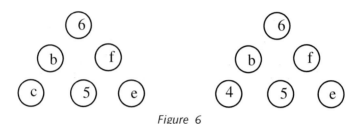

Figure 6

Where does the 4 go? Because of symmetry there are just two cases. Either $b = 4$ or $c = 4$. If $b = 4$, then $6 + b + c$ is greater than or equal to $6 + 4 + c$ which is at least 11. But $c + 5 + e$ is less than $3 + 5 + 2$ (or $2 + 5 + 3$) because the biggest numbers we've got left are 2 and 3. So $c + 5 + e$ isn't going to be bigger than 10. One side wants to be at least 11 while another is desperately trying to be no bigger than 10. Can't have that. So b can't be 4. That forces c to be 4.

Then b can't be 3 because $6 + 3 + 4 = 13$ and $4 + 5 + e$ is less than or equal to $4 + 5 + 2$ which is never bigger than 11. And $b \neq 2$, since $6 + 2 + 4 = 12$ and $6 + f + e = 6 + 1 + 3$ (or $6 + 3 + 1) = 10$. So b has to be 1. This forces $e = 2$ and $f = 3$. That looks familiar too.

Further Explorations

11. Check through the arguments of Cases 1.1, 1.2 and 1.3. Are you convinced so far? Can you find a quicker solution?

12. Now go on and check out Case 2 in the same way. Remember to use the symmetry to reduce the number of cases.

◆ ◆ ◆

Having exhausted all the possibilities with 6 in the corner, we've completed Case 1 with two successes and nothing new. What's the betting we're not going to find any more than four answers to the original question? Now for Case 2, and 6 on the side.

Case 2 Try b = 6. By symmetry 5 can be a, f or e.

Case 2.1 Put 5 in circle a first. This means that c must be 1 because otherwise 5 + 6 + c is greater than 12 and 5 + f + e is always less than or equal to 5 + 4 + 3 = 12. With c = 1, f and e must be 3 and 4 to give a side sum of 12. Hence d = 2. But then c + d + e must only be 7. We therefore can't get a solution with 5 in circle a.

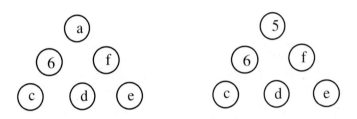

Figure 7

Case 2.2 Put 5 in f then. Now you can't put 4 in a because then a + 6 + c = 4 + 6 + c which is at least 11 and c + d + e = 1 + 2 + 3 which is only 6. If 4 goes in c, a + 6 + 4 is at least 11 and c + d + e is less than or equal to 4 + 2 + 3 = 9. So 4 has to go in d or e.

Figure 8

With 4 in d, then a = 1 forces an answer we've seen before. But c = 1 means a + 6 + 1 is at least 2 + 6 + 1 = 9, while c + 4 + e is never bigger than 1 + 4 + 3 = 8. And e ≠ 1 either, by a similar sort of argument. If we try 4 in e, we again have problems. So this case only gives one more answer.

Case 2.3 Try 5 in circle e. Are you betting on only four answers now?

Further Explorations

13. Complete Case 2.3 for yourself.

14. Do you notice any patterns among the four answers we've found? Could we use that to find the four answers more quickly?

15. Show that if you have an answer with a, c, e in the corners, then you can move all the numbers around one circle to give another answer. (This answer, of course, will have a, c, e in the middle circles of the triangle.)

16. Try putting 1, 2, 3 in the corner circles and see how easy it is to get an answer.

    Now try to find an answer with 4, 5, 6 in the corners.

    Do you get an answer with 1, 2, 4 in the corners? Why not?

17. Another approach to this problem is to list all the possible sets of three numbers and put them one by one in the corner circles. Try this and see how easy it is.

18. Use Exploration 15 to halve the number of cases you need to use in the new approach to the problem given in Exploration 17.

19. Can you find another way to solve this problem?

◆ ◆ ◆ ◆

OK. So we only found the same **four** answers that we had produced by guess work ages ago. Of course, now we have actually proved that there are precisely four answers to the original question. But was the effort really worth it? How does this help your Indy Anna-Jones? Will any of the four answers work for her? Maybe it really is time to take a break.

2. WHAT DOES IT MEAN "TO DO MATHEMATICS"?

So far we've looked at some classes doing mathematics. We've even done some maths ourselves. But what does that mean? Perhaps before we answer that we need to ask **who** does mathematics? Presumably almost everybody at some point in their lives. Do they all **do** maths the same way though? The accountant, the school student, the research mathematician, the person balancing their cheque book, do they all do the same thing, essentially?

Maybe we need to ask another question. What is mathematics?

First, what is the main aim of mathematics? Surely it's to make sense of, and understand, the world, in order to make informed decisions about it. In this aim mathematics is not alone. Surely this is the main goal of a good many disciplines and they each approach this goal in their own way. What makes mathematics different is that it is largely concerned with the **quantifiable** aspects of the world. Counting, of course, is basic to this, as is geometry. However, there are many aspects of mathematics which have developed from counting and geometry and now look nothing like their roots.

In practice, the subject mathematics has two main facets. It is a collection of skills and results that have been built up over the years, combined with a set of processes that enable new results to be obtained. We all know about the skills' and results' side because this is the aspect that has been the main function of the teaching of mathematics in schools and even in universities. Skills consist of such things as being able to add, subtract, divide and multiply with simple numbers, and knowing the algorithm to add, say, three-digit numbers. In the primary school not many results as such are taught but these consist of such things as the formula for the area of a circle and Pythagoras' Theorem about the square on the hypotenuse being equal to the sum of the squares on the other two sides.

There is not much that can be done in maths without using some skills or some previous results, so this is an important area of mathematics. Everybody, for example, uses arithmetic everyday. This is what the person balancing their cheque book is doing. If you bother to check your change, then you are doing arithmetic. Professionals use more complicated maths to do such diverse things as scheduling cabin crews for airliners and building bridges.

Surprisingly, the skills' area is one which is developing every day as research mathematicians invent or discover new things to add to the skills and results we already know. We want to emphasise this point. Mathematics is being produced "as we speak"! It is not a box of goodies that dropped to Earth out of a clear blue sky one day. Mathematics didn't come down on tablets of stone from the mountain, complete for all time. There are people out there right now, tackling new problems and producing more mathematics that can then be used by someone in the "real world" to do something useful or which can be used by another research mathematician to produce yet another skill or result. So this tells us something about research mathematicians. Some of them are trying to discover new things, things no one has thought of before. They do it for many reasons. For some, it's the sheer delight of discovery, like being the first person on top of Everest. For others, it's the hope of fame. For yet others, it's an interesting and challenging way of earning a living. And for some it's a combination of those and other things.

Mathematicians who are trying to find new results like this, or who are interested in maths for its own sake, are often referred to as Pure Mathematicians. On the other hand, Applied Mathematicians are mathematicians whose main concern is to apply mathematics to some practical area. This involves them more in solving real questions than in producing new results that someone else might use.

Applied mathematicians are involved in scheduling cabin crews, trying to produce models which will explain the weather or the economy, or simply balancing a cheque book. But almost everyone who is using mathematics is doing so because they have a question they want to answer. The only difference between pure and applied mathematicians is that one has an abstract question and the other has a practical question.

Further Explorations

20. Make a list of six types of people you know who use mathematics in different ways. Which of these would you call pure mathematicians and which applied mathematicians? Is it possible for someone to be a pure mathematician one minute and an applied mathematician the next?

21. What topics in school maths do you think are pure and which applied? Is everything potentially pure? Is everything potentially applied?

◆ ◆ ◆ ◆

This seemingly endless supply of knowledge that some people are producing, is one important reason for mathematicians to talk to each other and to read books, or at least to know where the material can be found. They never know when some new result may help them to solve a problem that they are currently working on. So to let everyone else know what they have done, they try to have it published in specialized research journals. One of the problems with that is, that the results are written up in a very drab, professional way. The emphasis is on giving the result and providing a proof, rather than giving any idea of the way that the result was obtained. As a result the creative processes are omitted. This is not really a difficulty for professionals. After all, they should have a pretty good idea of how original ideas are obtained. The real problem is that lecturers at university tend to adopt the same dry form of presentation. This then tends to get repeated in university texts and then school texts. The secondary school teachers who have been brought up through this dry but rigorous process, tend to teach in the same way. Along the way, the whole excitement of discovery has been lost. It would be nice if that creative spirit could somehow find its way into the maths that's done at school.

But mathematicians also talk to themselves a lot. One of the key things about doing maths is talking to yourself and asking yourself questions. By asking the right questions you lead yourself to the right answer (hopefully). The trick is to know how to ask these questions. What you have to do is to make the questions answerable. The general idea is to break down all the big questions into manageable pieces. That way you can end up answering the big questions. Of course, that's not as easily said as done. But it's one of the things that we hope you will learn through working through this book. It's what we already did in order to get a solution to the buttons' problem and the seating problem. But we're getting a bit ahead of ourselves. Basically everyone who uses mathematics is a mathematician. And mathematicians use mathematics to answer questions. You may have noticed that we have talked about "answering questions" rather than "solving problems". The point is that many questions we tackle are not problems. We know ahead of time what strategy to use. With the cheque book, we know we have to use arithmetic and it's usually addition or subtraction that we need. In this book there may not be too many questions but there will be many problems.

But apart from skills and results, there is the process of mathematics. We'll get back to that in a later chapter.

Further Explorations

22. Name six people who were famous because they made some advance in mathematics. When and where did they live and what piece of mathematics made them famous? Include at least two women in your six.

23. Noether, Turing, Gödel and Julia were all mathematicians who worked this century. Which was a woman and which had no nose? What areas of mathematics did they contribute to?

24. Name two applications of mathematics in every day life where multiplication is required.

25. Apart from builders, who uses geometry?

26. How do builders use Pythagoras' Theorem?

3. CIRCLES AGAIN

While we've been talking about mathematicians, deep in our brain we've been thinking about that circles problem again. Incidentally, it's worth pointing out that thinking goes on all the time whether we like it or not, and we seem to be able to think about a number of things at once. There appears to be a lot of activity going on in the brain that we have no control over. Consequently, when we are doing maths, or anything else for that matter, we won't always have control over what we are doing. That often means that we will have several ideas all at once that may be worth processing. As a result, doing maths problems is very seldom a linear affair. It is unusual in problem solving to start at the beginning, know what to do next, and then follow it through to a conclusion. Almost always, there will be different ideas to sift through and decide which one to follow. The problem is that no one particular idea may be the absolute best. Two or three of them may get you to the solution eventually.

So what was it about the circles problem that our brain was working on, while we were thinking about other things? Well, it occurred to us that it might be of some value to add all the numbers in the circles. After all that would nearly be three times the sum on any one side. The difference would be just the numbers on the corners because the sum of the three sides counts the corners twice. So, three times the numbers on any one side is precisely equal to the sum of all the numbers from 1 to 6, plus whatever numbers there are at the corners. Now the numbers from 1 to 6 add up to 21. What use this is likely to be is not clear at the moment but hopefully it might lead somewhere. It would be nice if it led to a better proof than the systematic search did. After all that did seem to get somewhat tedious with all its cases.

So we have

three times the side sum   = sum of 1 to 6 + all the corner numbers
                             = 21 + all the corner numbers

What does that tell us? This method might be worth pursuing if we could find the corner numbers easily. Why? Hmm, where would we be if we could find the corner numbers? We'd know three times the sum of any side. So? That would tell us the sum of one side. So? Ah. If we knew the sum and the corner numbers, then it would be simple to fit in all the other numbers. See, if the corner numbers were 1, 2, 3 and the sum was 9, then on the 1 and 2 side we'd put in 6, on the 2 and 3 side we'd put in 4 and on the 1 and 3 side we'd add in 5. Knowing the corner numbers would pretty well finish off the whole problem! Wait on, it's even better than that. If we knew the corner numbers, then the equation we worked out above would give us three times the side sum and hence the side sum. Knowing the corner numbers actually forces the side sum and then the remaining numbers **have** to fall in place. Knowing the corner numbers essentially solves the whole problem for us. Let's find those corner numbers then.

What have we got to go on? The only thing that we actually know about the corner numbers is that

three times the side sum   = 21 + all the corner numbers.

So,

all the corner numbers   = three times the side sum - 21.

But what does that tell us? Not much. Well, the right hand side of that equation is divisible by three. That means that the sum of the corner numbers is too. Is that any help? How many lots of three numbers out of the numbers from 1 to 6, give sums divisible by three? 1, 2, 3 do. So do 1, 3, 5. Looks as if there are going to be a lot. Can we list them all systematically? Why not start from the smallest and work up. That way we'll get

1, 2, 3	1, 2, 6	1, 3, 5	1, 5, 6
2, 3, 4	2, 4, 6	3, 4, 5	4, 5, 6.

That looks like all of them. Hang on though. That suggests that we will get eight answers and so far we have only found four. Where have we gone wrong? Let's sort that out later. What do these corner numbers give us?

Further Exploration

27. Try each of these corner numbers and find out which ones work and which don't. Why are there only four answers?

Bingo! That seems a nice way of getting four answers. And once we got the idea sorted out it was a lot quicker than the systematic search we went through earlier! Do you begin to see what we mean by "better" solutions?

4. AN INVESTIGATION

But why restrict ourselves to the numbers 1, 2, 3, 4, 5, 6 in the original problem? Can we get four answers with **any** six consecutive integers? Are there non-consecutive integers that will do the job? Is it possible to find general sets of six distinct numbers with $a + b + c = c + d + e = e + f + a$? For any such set, will there be four answers? Will these four answers be somehow related to the four answers which use the first six digits?

Further Explorations

28. Which of the following sets of numbers work?

   (i)   1, 2, 3, 4, 5, 7;   (ii)   4, 5, 6, 10, 11, 12;
   (iii)   1, 2, 3, 15, 16, 17;   (iv)   1, 2, 3, 4, 5, 8.

29. Write down six numbers which obviously **don't** work.

30. Does every set of six numbers that works, give four different answers?

You can see that we've gone into investigation mode. We're already **extending** the original Indy problem. Maybe we can generalise it later. After all, the obvious question now is what six numbers can we place in the circles so that the sums of the numbers on each of the three sides of the triangle are the same? If we could achieve a solution to this problem we would have a **generalization** of the original problem. This is because the original problem would just be a special case of the problem we have just posed.

Just to amplify that a bit. Suppose that we found that the only way that six numbers would fit in the circles with the required equal sums, is if they were all consecutive. Then since any six consecutive numbers would work, then the special case of the numbers 1 to 6 would have to work too. The original circles problem would have been generalised.

You probably have to do a bit of experimentation to see what progress you can make with the general problem: what can be said about six numbers if when placed in the circles, the sums of the numbers on each side are equal? We'll wait for you. Try to produce as many sets of six numbers as you can and then see if there is some pattern. Start from what you know already.

Further Explorations

31. What do you think of the conjecture that if six numbers fit in the circles in the appropriate way, then they have to be consecutive?

32. On the other hand, show that any six consecutive numbers will fit into the circles so that the sums of the numbers on each of the three sides are the same.

    How many ways can this be done?

◆ ◆ ◆ ◆

We're starting to get into heavy language weather here. If we keep on having to say, put the six number in the circles that are arranged in such and such a way, so that the sums are this and that, we're going to bore ourselves to tears. So let's agree to say that six numbers are nice if they can be put, one each to a circle, so that the sums of the numbers on each side of the triangle are the same. You can see that the numbers 1, 2, 3, 4, 5, 6 are nice. But then any six consecutive numbers are nice.

Now it's worth noting what you probably came up with fairly quickly, that if all six numbers are the same, then there is no difficulty balancing the side sums. As all six numbers in our original problem were different, perhaps we should impose that restraint on the general problem too. So nice numbers have to all be different.

Now what examples can you come up with? Did you get anything like the answer in Figure 9? Is there any sense in which the nice numbers (2, 4, 6, 8, 10, 12) in Figure 9 represent anything new?

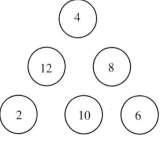

Figure 9

Starting from a known answer (the middle one in Figure 3), we've got another answer just by doubling the numbers.

Further Explorations

33. Starting with the nice numbers 1, 2, 3, 4, 5, 6, can you generate a whole lot of other nice numbers?
34. Starting with six consecutive nice numbers, generate one hundred more lots of nice numbers.

35. Can you find other ways of getting nice numbers from some known nice numbers?
36. Can you generate another set of nice numbers from two different lots of nice numbers?

37. Will every set of nice numbers produce four different answers?

38. Can you prove all the things you have conjectured about nice numbers?

Imagine starting those last exercises correctly and precisely without having defined nice numbers. That's why we have definitions in maths. It makes communication that much easier. When you think about it we could have used any word we like in place of "nice". So long as we defined it precisely we could have used "circular", "pretty", "triangular", or whatever else we liked. Actually "circular" or "triangular" might have been better than nice. They are more related to the problem. It does sometimes help to remember the defined word, and what it means, if it has something to do with the situation we're working with.

Anyway, we've seen how to produce new sets of nice numbers by multiplying a given set of nice numbers by any number we choose. We can also generate new nice numbers by adding some constant to some known nice numbers. Figure 10 gives us an example of this. By adding 12 to each of the numbers in the last diagram in Figure 3, we get the answer shown in Figure 10.

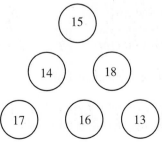

Figure 10

But if you can multiply nice numbers by any number or if you can add any fixed number to some answer, surely you can do a combination of the two. If we start with the answer in Figure 2 and multiply every number by 5 and then add 3, we get the answer in Figure 11.

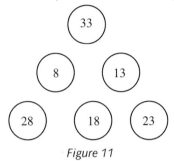

Figure 11

So it looks as if every set of six numbers that can be obtained from the numbers 1 to 6 by first multiplying by some fixed number and then adding any fixed number, can be put into circles. Such sets are said to be linear combinations of the numbers 1 to 6. It's not too hard to show that sets which are **linear combinations** of 1 to 6 are themselves nice numbers.

Further Explorations

39. Can you prove that any linear combination of the numbers 1 to 6 gives a set of nice numbers?

40. Is a linear combination of a linear combination of some set of numbers, simply just one linear combination of that set of numbers?

    (Try a few examples.)

41. Is every nice lot of numbers a linear combination of 1, 2, 3, 4, 5, 6?

42. Which of the following sets of numbers are nice?

    (i)   1, 2, 3, 99, 100, 101;   (ii)   1, 5, 51, 52, 55, 102;
    (iii)   1, 5, 51, 55, 100, 150;   (iv)   1, 5, 90, 92, 94, 181;
    (v)   1, 5, 90, 94, 106, 110;   (vi)   1, 5, 10, 16, 22, 29.

    How many nice numbers give four answers?

43. In the last Exploration we have given each of the five possible types of nice numbers. Can you distinguish each of these types?

44. Rewrite the Temple of Gloom problem in a more interesting context.

5. CHAPTER SUMMARY

In this chapter we used the following strategies:

> guess and check;
> be systematic;
> use a diagram;
> use algebra;
> use symmetry.

We thought about what mathematics is and what mathematicians, both pure and applied, do. We also thought again about the idea of an investigation as an extended piece of problem solving. Investigations frequently use extensions and generalizations. We also mentioned, the value of introducing a definition to cut down the amount of words required to explain what is going on.

CHAPTER 7   SNAKEYES

1. A DICE PROBLEM

Snakeye Sam had been running his illegal craps game behind the big lecture theatre at the college of education for just over 30 years. But he had been slowing down lately. He can't figure out the odds as quickly as he used to. He found it hard to remember the chances of getting seven when rolling two dice. Why was it easier to get a total of six rather than a total of twelve? Heck. Life would be a lot easier if all the totals came up equally often. So he set about designing a pair of dice so that each of the sums 1, 2, ..., 12 were equally likely. Was that possible? Could it be done? How?

Sam scratched his head and started to figure it out. There was a lot that was unstated here. He obviously didn't have to worry about what sums he was thinking about. Everyone knows that when two dice land they have to land flat (neither of them is allowed to be caught edge on), and that the sum is the sum of the dots (or numbers) on the top face.

What else is unstated? Well, everyone knows that normal dice are cube-shaped and cubes have six faces. A normal die (the singular of dice is die though goodness knows why) has the numbers 1 to 6, one on each face. And the normal die has the 1 and 6 on opposite faces, the 2 and 5 on opposite faces, and the 3 and 4 on opposite faces. Now, perhaps not everyone knows that last fact. You might check it out. But it was meat and drink to Sam. Having got that far though, Sam wondered whether, once the 1 and 6 are in place, there was only one way to put the other numbers on the die so that the numbers on opposite faces sum to 7. Or is there a left handed and right handed form? Or were there more than two ways of finishing the die?

Further Explorations

1. Show that there are exactly two ways of making a die using the numbers 1 to 6, so that the sum of the numbers on opposite sides of the die is always 7. (Note that one of these is the "Western" die used in casinos and the other is the "Eastern" die to be found in all Mahjong sets.)

   Make these two different dice. Do they have the same probability properties? Would the Easter die cause havoc at the casino?

2. If you don't insist that the numbers on opposite sides of the die add up to 7, how many possible dice are there?

◆ ◆ ◆ ◆

Before we go on we'd like you to make a note of the things that you can't understand, are unable to do for yourself, or any other difficulty you have in the course of this chapter. At the end of the chapter we'll get you to analyse this list.

So, given your two normal dice, anyone who has ever played Monopoly or Backgammon knows that you can't throw a 1. The sum of the numbers on the tops of the two dice won't make 1 no matter how hard you try. So these two dice Sam was trying to make must be special in some way. But maybe not too special. After all, regular dice can produce all the other sums from two up to twelve.

Now Sam wondered whether it went any further than that? Are there any other differences between normal dice and the ones he was trying to invent. With normal dice, are the chances of getting each total from 2 to 12 equally likely? What does that mean? What is the chance of throwing a 2 anyway? At one stage in his life Snakeye could have just snapped back an answer to that. Somehow these days he wasn't in to snapping.

Further Explorations

3.   How many ways are there of getting a total of 3 with two normal dice?

4.   How many ways are there of getting a total of 7 with two normal dice?

5.   Is it true that there are as many ways of getting 2 as there are of getting 12? What about 3 and 11, 4 and 10, and so on?

         How many ways are there of getting 6 with three dice?

Well, of course there's actually only one **way** of getting a 2. One die rolls a 1 and so does the other. So are the **chances** of getting a 2 just one? What does that mean? There is a convention surrounding probabilities, chances. The number one represents certainty, the probability that something **must** happen. The number zero means that something can **not** happen. So every probability is a number between zero and one inclusive. For probabilities between zero and one we use fractions, decimals and, sometimes, percentages. So if the chances of getting 2 are just one, then it's not possible to get any other totals.

When you think about it, there are not too many things that are certainties. "The Sun will rise tomorrow". Hopefully yes. But given the mechanics of the Universe as we currently understand them, one day the Sun won't rise. When will we know to reduce the probabilities from one to something slightly less?

"The probability that at least one horse will finish the race", Sam thought. Probably yes. But it is possible that they'll all fall over or that some other catastrophe will stop the event. After all, he remembered one Grand National a few years ago that was stopped and declared a no-race. Who would have bet on that possibility?

On the other hand, if two normal dice are rolled and they both land flat on the tables, then certainly the total of the two dice will be one of 2, 3, 4, 5, 6, 7, 8, 9, 10, 11 or 12. This happens with a probability of one.

Now Sam's problem talks about each sum occurring with equal probability. Each sum has to have the same chance of occurring. Does this happen with two normal dice? Would you expect the sum 11 to turn up as often as 4, for example? He suspected that there might be a difference. After all, a double 6 occurred on only rare occasions.

He started to do a little analysis. How can I get a sum of 2? Surely there's only one way: 1 + 1. What about 4? Well, I can get 4 by 1 + 3 or by 2 + 2. So 4 must come up more often than 2. But how more often? Clearly it's at least twice as often. Are there ways of getting 4 that we haven't listed?

Sam wondered what would happen if he had one die coloured white and the other red. Then he could get 4 if the white die showed 1 and the red die shows 3. Is this the same as the white die showing 3 and the red die 1? No. So here are two ways of getting 4 so far.

The only other way to get 4 is via 2 and 2. Can 2 and 2 come in two ways? After all, he had managed to get 1 and 3 two ways. Is 2 on the white die plus 2 on the red, the same as 2 on the red die plus 2 on the white? Obviously, yes. So the 2 + 2 option can only occur once.

Altogether then, he was satisfied that there are three ways of getting 4. They are, essentially, 1 + 3, 3 + 1, 2 + 2. So 4 will come up three times as often as 2.

Further Explorations

6. How many ways are there of getting a sum of 6 using two normal dice?

7. Which sum is most likely to occur when two normal dice are rolled?

8. Which sum is the least likely to occur when two normal dice are rolled? (Is this a catch question?)

◆ ◆ ◆ ◆

Knowing how often any given sum appears, however, will not tell you the chances of that sum actually appearing. There is a difference between frequency of occurrence and probability of occurrence. In fact

$$\text{probability of occurrence} = \frac{\text{frequency of occurrence}}{\text{number of total possible occurrences}}$$

For instance what's the probability of throwing a 6 when rolling a single die? How many ways can you get a 6? Just once. How many possible numbers can come up when rolling a die? Six – there's just one number on each face. So that

$$\text{probability of throwing a 6} = \frac{\text{number of ways of getting a 6}}{\text{number of possible numbers}}$$

$$= \frac{1}{6}.$$

In the same way, the probability of throwing either a 5 or 6 is $\frac{2}{6}\left(=\frac{1}{3}\right)$. You can only get 5 and 6 one way each.

With two dice, things are a little more interesting. What's the probability of throwing a sum of 2 using two dice?

$$\text{probability of a sum of 2} = \frac{\text{number of ways of getting a 2}}{\text{number of ways of getting any sum}}$$

We know that there is only one way of getting 2 (1 + 1). How many possible outcomes are there when two dice are rolled? How could we work that out?

Suppose the white die showed a 1. Then the red die might be any one of 1, 2, 3, 4, 5, 6. So there are six ways of rolling the dice so that the white die showed 1.

Suppose the white die showed a 2. Again the red die might turn up in any one of 6 ways.

Suppose the white die showed ... Hang on. Surely whatever the white die showed, the red die could show any of 6 numbers. How many numbers could the white die show? Six. So there must be 6 sums for each of the 6 ways the white die could roll. That gives 36 possible outcomes when two dice are rolled. Hence

$$\text{probability of a sum of 2} = \frac{1}{36}.$$

Further Explorations

9. Find the probabilities of getting each of the following sums when two normal dice are rolled.

   (i) 3;   (ii) 6;   (iii) 9;   (iv) 12.

10. What sum(s) occurs with probability $\dfrac{1}{6}$ when two normal die are rolled?

11. Which is more likely to occur, a sum of 6 or less, or a sum of 9 or more? (A sum of 6 or less includes sums of 2, 3, 4, 5 and 6.)

12. What is the probability of getting a head when you flip a fair coin?

13. What is the probability of getting two heads when you toss two coins simultaneously?

14. What is the probability of getting a tail and a 4 when you simultaneously toss a coin and roll a die?

◆ ◆ ◆ ◆

A grid provides a useful way of looking at the outcome of two regular dice (see Figure 1). From the body of the grid, we can see that 5 occurs four times. Hence the probability of getting a sum of 5 is

$$\frac{4}{36} = \frac{1}{9}.$$

red

		1	2	3	4	5	6
	1	2	3	4	5	6	7
	2	3	4	5	6	7	8
white	3	4	5	6	7	8	9
	4	5	6	7	8	9	10
	5	6	7	8	9	10	11
	6	7	8	9	10	11	12

Figure 1

All this reinforces the fact that not all of the sums from 2 to 12 are equally likely when two normal dice are rolled. Sam had known that all along. Does it seem possible therefore that he could put new numbers on these dice so that the sums from 1 to 12, inclusive, had the same probability of occurring?

It's worth having a guess at this stage. What does your intuition tell you? Of course, if you say "yes", then you have to produce two dice that would do the job. If you say "no", then you've got to give a pretty good reason why. What do you think? Is it easier to make two dice or find out why they couldn't exist? Snakeye Sam didn't know the answer to that question.

Further Exploration

15. Spend a little time trying to solve the problem of producing two dice which will give equi-probable totals from 1 to 12, inclusive. (We don't expect you to read on until you've either solved the problem or devoted at least 30 minutes to it. If you think you've solved the problem, then convince your father, a friend or the cat, that you have. If your cat is not convinced, write your argument down on paper.)

◆ ◆ ◆

We're not really sure how to vote ourselves. In a problem like this, though, where we've got no insight, it's probably easiest to try to make two dice that will do the job. There's a chance we may be able to construct them by wildcatting or by trial and error. If we can't manage to come up with dice that do the trick, we may find a reason for them not existing in the process. It's a bit "hit and hope" but Snakeye seems to have no clues, so here goes.

We're going to guess that it can be done. (This is largely because we are more confident that we can construct things than we are that we can prove that something can't happen.) So if we want to be sophisticated about this we'll call it a conjecture rather than a guess.

Conjecture. Two dice **can** be labelled so that every sum from 1 to 12, inclusive is equally likely.

Having jumped that way what does this tell us? If there are two such dice, what else can be said? The point of asking those questions is that they might lead us to a clue that will help us in some way. If we ask finer and finer questions we may be able to solve enough of them to get an answer to the big question.

The Conjecture has a few different aspects. How can we use them? It seems to us there are three key pieces of information. First of all there are **two dice**, not one, three or a hundred. Then we are to get every sum from **1 to 12**. So, we **can** get 1. This is unlike normal dice where the lowest number we can get is 2. The third key piece of information is that all outcomes are **equally likely.** There's no joy in being able to get all sums from 1 to 12 if 7 occurs more often than 5. The probability of each sum must be exactly the same.

So we've got two dice. How can we get all sums from 1 to 12? How can we get 1 for a start?

Further Explorations

16. OK, so how can we get 1?

17. How can we get 2? What about 5; 9; 12?

What are the rules here? Can we use fractions? Are negative numbers allowed? Would it be OK to use a zero, say?

Unfortunately the question is delightfully vague on this point. Could we get 1 using $\frac{1}{2} + \frac{1}{2}$, 924 + (–923) or 0 + 1?

We're afraid it's up to us. In a situation like this we're on our own. Snakeye has gone into a deep reverie. It's no good asking him. We have to make a decision and stick to it until it either works or until we get so frustrated we go back and try again or give up.

Before we plump for one or the other, let's just see where we've got to. We've summarized progress so far in Figure 2.

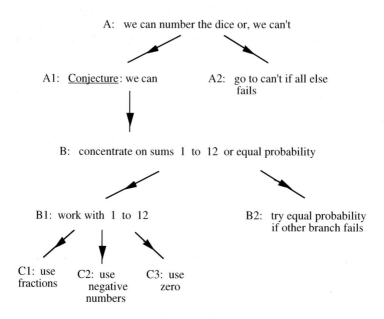

A: we can number the dice or, we can't

A1: Conjecture: we can

A2: go to can't if all else fails

B: concentrate on sums 1 to 12 or equal probability

B1: work with 1 to 12

B2: try equal probability if other branch fails

C1: use fractions

C2: use negative numbers

C3: use zero

A decision tree for the dice problem

Figure 2

You can see that we've been progressing down a tree diagram. We're gradually working on what we hope are smaller and smaller problems. One reason for thinking about things this way is that, if we get stuck, we can always go back to some previous branching point and start again. Hopefully, we might have more luck that way. If not, we can always go back to some previously explored branch in the hope that we'll find something we missed last time. The diagram that we've started making could be called a **decision tree**.

We're going to use a zero. If the branch fails, C3 in Figure 1, we can always try C1 or C2. In this case then, one die must have a zero and the other a 1. (See Figure 3.)

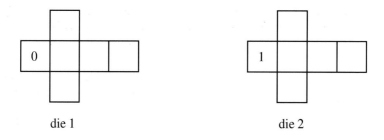

die 1   die 2

Figure 3

Further Exploration

18. Now that we've got a total of 1, how can we get a sum of 2? How about a sum of 3? Don't stop there.

◆ ◆ ◆ ◆

If we're going to go down this path, that is, the path of constructing the dice "with our bare hands", then we've got to put some system into it. If we don't, we'll lose sight of what we're doing. What's worse, we might miss finding the dice we're after. Here's one way of trying to be systematic.

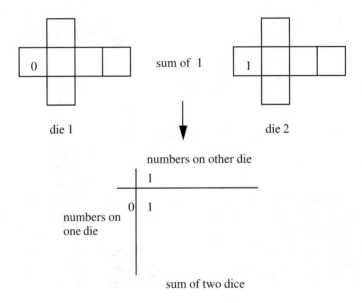

Figure 4

So how could we get a 2 then? There seem to be two ways. They're shown in Figure 5. We've put there the tables that are produced as a result of the two pairs of dice.

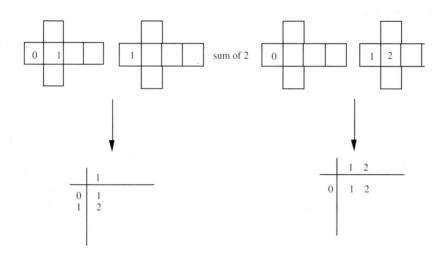

Figure 5

But then things are starting to get out of hand (see Figure 6). The number of possibilities starts to proliferate at a great old rate. Though some possibilities do occur on both sides and some of these possibilities are not too bad. But things like 0,1 and 1,2 are a worry because they give us a sum of 2 by either 1+1 or 0+2. While we know that we need more than one way of getting 2. Or do we?

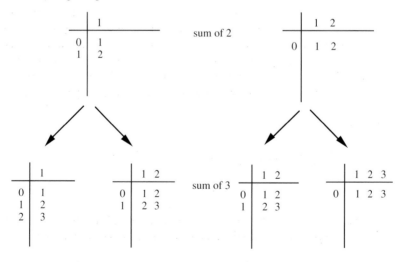

Figure 6

Further Exploration

19. How many ways must we get 2 on Snakeye's dice? How many ways must we get every other sum from 1 to 12? How do we know we must get them that many ways?

◆ ◆ ◆ ◆

The reason we've stopped in our tracks for a bit is that systematically exploring all the possibilities as we were doing in Figure 6 looked as if it was going to get out of hand. It's a bit like trying all possible ways of putting the numbers 1 to 6 in the circles in the Temple of Gloom problem. It could certainly be done. We might even have managed to programme a computer to do it. However, there was a nice way to speed up the process for Indy Anna-Jones and get us home before tea time. Can we speed up the process here? Do we have a piece of information that we haven't yet used?

Further Exploration

20. What piece of information has yet to be used? How can it be used? What will it tell us?

◆ ◆ ◆ ◆

While you're thinking about that it may be worth looking at the "top" end. How can we expect to get a sum of 12? Could we have 12 + 0, for instance? That would tell us that on the die which had 0, all of the other numbers would have to be 0 or negative, otherwise, we'd find a sum **greater** than 12. It's not likely that all zeros on one die will work. We could only come up with six different possible totals this way - not the twelve possibilities that we need. And we decided against negative numbers at step C3 in Figure 1. If we stick with C3 then, there's at least a limit to the size of number that we can put on these dice.

Further Exploration

21. What is the biggest number that we can have on either die?

◆ ◆ ◆ ◆

Hang on. Maybe we can use the fact that all outcomes are equally likely. We haven't used that yet. If we do, maybe we'll reduce the systematic search we started in Figure 4.

What does "all outcomes equally likely" tell us? Can we work out exactly how many times a sum of 1 occurs? Maybe, first of all we had better remember how many ways two sides, one on each die, can come up. The answer to that must be 6 ¥ 6 = 36. We did that earlier.

There are 36 outcomes. Now we want twelve sums to be equally possible, so each sum must have to happen exactly three times.

The result of that little calculation is that a sum of 1 must come up **three** times. How can we manage that? If we're sticking with $0 + 1 = 1$, perhaps we can list all the ways that three 1s are possible. We've tried to do that, as systematically as we can, in Figure 7.

(i)	0; and 1,1,1	(ii)	0,0; and 1,1
(iii)	0,0,0; and 1	(iv)	0,1; and 0,1,1
(v)	0,0; and 0,1,1	any more?	

Figure 7

We'd better check these out because some of them look a bit worrying. That number (ii) suggestion, for instance is a bit of a problem. Doesn't that give us four sums of 1? And numbers (iv) and (v) gives sums of 0. We certainly don't want that. Then (i) and (iii) seem to be the only possibilities. So which one will we push on with? OK, let's try (i).

If we say that there's one 0 on the first die and three 1s on the other, how do we get three sums of 2? I suppose the easiest way is to put a 1 on the first die. This gives us Figure 8. Bingo! Threes 2s straight off!

$$\begin{array}{c|ccc} & 1 & 1 & 1 \\ \hline 0 & 1 & 1 & 1 \\ 1 & 2 & 2 & 2 \\ \end{array}$$

Figure 8

Now surely the easiest way to get three 3s is to put a 2 on the first die (see Figure 9). Looking good!

$$\begin{array}{c|ccc} & 1 & 1 & 1 \\ \hline 0 & 1 & 1 & 1 \\ 1 & 2 & 2 & 2 \\ 2 & 3 & 3 & 3 \\ \end{array}$$

Figure 9

Further Explorations

22. When you're on a good thing, stick to it. So finish off the problem.

23. We got as far as the last Exploration by using alternative (i) in Figure 5. What happens if we work with alternative (iii)? Can we solve the problem this way too?

24. Are there any other ways of numbering this dice? Are there any ways of using C1 or C2 from Figure 2.

25. How many answers are there to this problem?

26. Can you rouse Snakeye and tell him the good news?

2. HOW DO THEY DO IT?

In Chapter 2 we talked about mathematicians and what they do. At a superficial level we talked about how they did it. But we didn't really pursue how research mathematicians do what they do.

The bit of mathematics which is not just skills and results, and how to use them is called **process**. This is the way old things are put together to form new things. We're going to talk in a minute about research mathematicians and the way they use process. But mathematical process, used in exactly the same way that research mathematicians use it, is used by many people.

Even New Entrants can use process. It may not lead them to results which are new on a world scale but the result will be new for them. The joy of discovery will be just as great for someone cracking the Mothers' Day card problem for the first time as it will for an Einstein seeing something **completely** new that no one else has ever seen before.

Every mathematician starts with a problem. What often happens next is an intense period where lots of examples are worked out to get some idea of how the problem behaves and to get some understanding of the ins and outs of the problem. This is a period of **experimentation** similar to that employed by chemists and biologists and other research scientists.

From all these experiments the mathematicians get some feel for what is going on. They then produce a guess as to the nature of the solution. Because mathematicians are sophisticated people, they don't admit to guessing. They call their guesses **conjectures** but they are guesses just the same, guesses built on their experience and insight.

The next step in the process is to try to determine how good the conjectures are. If they are good, then the hope is to **prove** them. This is a very important aspect of mathematics. Within mathematics we are able to prove things. This is not the case to the same extent in any other discipline. In physics, for instance, there are only theories that are "proved" by experience and experiment. Given a more refined experiment or new circumstances, the theories may change. An example of this is the gradual perception of the Solar System. Initially it was thought that it was all on the backs of turtles, then it was thought that the Earth was at the centre, and so on. In mathematics then, proven things are true for all time. No new experiment can change them.

The other thing to note about proofs is that there may be more than one way of proving results. Surprisingly mathematicians have a fetish for proving things in the nicest way they can. Why is this so? It is hard to say but it has become part of the mathematical culture. At your next party try to catch two mathematicians talking in the corner. Listen to them drool over "nice" solutions, an "elegant" piece of work, and "pretty" arguments.

Should a proof be produced, then the next step is to try to find a **generalization** or in some way to **extend** the problem. The generalisation route leads us off to try to find a bigger problem which has the original problem as a special case. From there, we go onto the next problem and start all over again.

Now not every conjecture can be proved. Probably the vast majority of conjectures turn out to be false. Some of them can be altered slightly to make them true. Others can't. One quick way of establishing that a conjecture is false, is to find a **counterexample**. A counterexample is an example which does not satisfy the conjecture.

Having struck a counterexample, we may go on to a new problem or do some more experimentation to get a better conjecture. Actually, sometimes the counterexample will suggest how the first conjecture should be adjusted. Then the new conjecture has to be proved or counterexampled.

In the process of proving that a conjecture is true, mathematicians often oscillate between trying to find a proof and trying to find a counterexample. If they can't do either then they have to **give up**. This isn't a sin. Life is too short to try to solve all the conjectures of history. There are a number of very famous conjectures that we still are unable to settle either way. No one has either a proof or a counterexample. Giving up has to be a realistic strategy in the mathematician's arsenal.

One of these conjectures was suggested by Goldbach in 1742. He thought that every integer bigger than 5 could be written as the sum of three primes. For instance, $15 = 3 + 5 + 7$, $16 = 2 + 3 + 11$ and $17 = 3 + 3 + 11$. Despite progress in many areas in the last 350 or so years, we still can't prove or find a counterexample to Goldbach's conjecture. Many people have had to give up on this one.

However, giving up may sometimes lead to a solution. People have found that after a long period of banging their heads against a mathematical brick wall, if they stop working on the problem, a method of solution or at least an idea of how to proceed, suddenly pops into their heads. Of course, this doesn't always happen. But if you have really been struggling with something for a while without success, try giving up. There's a chance that your brain will still be working even if you don't think that it is. It's amazing the number of people who suddenly wake up in the middle of the night with the answer to their mathematical prayers.

But what does a mathematician do if the problem has **really** proved too hard? If even giving up for a while has been fruitless? They simply go on to some other problem (or retire). Then the whole process starts over again. This process is illustrated in Figure 10.

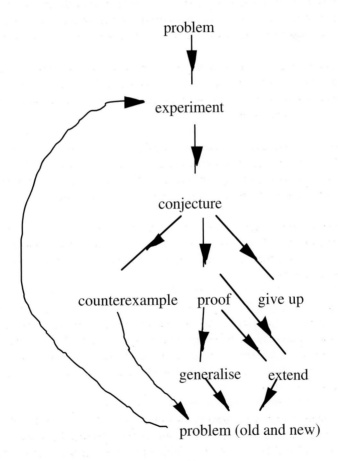

Figure 10

This diagram should look decidedly familiar. It's precisely what we said was a model for problem solving in Chapter 6. Is there no difference then between the processes that mathematicians use when they are doing research and the ones children use when they are problem solving? Essentially no. As is probably obvious, these processes are not as refined in problem solving students but the essential steps are precisely the same.

This even goes down to "nice" solutions and "elegant" pieces of work. You will remember that Fiona found a "nice" way of solving the Mothers' Day card problem when she removed 15 pence from the £1.25 and divided the remaining £1.10 equally between Matt and Sara. There was nothing wrong with making a table or using money or using rods or whatever. It is just that Fiona's method came out of the blue. Somehow it was unexpected. It was the sort of solution that you always wish **you** had thought of first.

Although the actual **processes** of research mathematics and problem solving are the same, clearly research mathematicians can do more complicated mathematics. Partly though, this is only a matter of experience. With practice, people get better at problem solving.

In this context, let's think about the Mothers' Day card problem again. There are two key aspects to this problem. One is the sum - two amounts add to £1.25, the other is the difference - two amounts differ by 15p. Young children, and novice problem solvers find it difficult to hold these two pieces of information in their heads at the one time. Hence they concentrate on one to the exclusion of the other. With practice, you can gradually get to hold the full picture in your head at one time so that all of the information is considered. It does take practice though. That is why one step problems should be worked on first. As these are mastered you can move children along to multi-step problems.

Further Explorations

27. Give two examples of "nice" or "elegant" solutions of a problem we have met.

28. Give some examples of one step problems, where only one piece of information has to be held in the head.

29. Give some examples of multi-step problems.

◆ ◆ ◆ ◆

Although problem solving in school is done more or less the way research mathematicians do research, there are a couple of ways in which they differ.

The first obvious differences are in the problems themselves. In problem solving, it's almost 100% certain that someone has solved the problem before the children are let loose on it. Almost certainly the teacher knows the answer or knows where to find the answer.

This is not the case with research mathematicians. They are not really doing research if they are trying to solve a problem that has already been solved.

The other difference with the problem is its importance. In school problem solving exercises, the problem may be interesting but solving it will not lead on to anything dramatically new. Research mathematics is quite different. There is the expectation that answers to research questions will enable us to do something that couldn't be done before. Some of these things even have an immediate impact and application.

The other thing about problem solving is that problems have usually been invented by someone else. In research mathematics, they may have been invented by the people who worked on them. On the other hand, many important problems have not been solved by their inventors and have been passed along from mathematician to mathematician. Some of them have been solved, some haven't.

We did say "usually the problems have been invented by someone else". In the sort of investigation that we got into with the Temple of Gloom problem, children may produce questions that no one else has thought of before. Maybe this will happen with Snakeye's problem as we move into the next section.

3. INVESTIGATION TIME

Where were we with the dice? Following on from Figure 9, you probably came up with the two dice

1, 1, 1, 7, 7, 7   and   0, 1, 2, 3, 4, 5.

But would you have come up with that one by yourself? Would you have worked systematically the way we did in Section 1 or would you have trialled and errored?

Or did you come up with

1, 1, 1, 4, 4, 4   and   0, 1, 2, 6, 7, 8

after working on from Figure 9? You might have got both! What other possibilities are there? How will we know when we've got them all?

Further Explorations

30. Are there any more solutions of the form

1, 1, 1, -, -, -   and   0, 1, 2, -, -, -?

31. Are there any different solutions of the form

    1, 1, 1, -, -, -   and   0, -, -, -, -, -?

32. Are there any solutions different to those in the last two Explorations?

Going back to Figure 7 we see that the only way to get three ones using the 0 + 1 technique is to have one zero on one die and three ones on the other, or one one on one die and three zeros on the other. Every other combination gives not enough ones or too many zeros or some such.

Take the one zero and three ones. How do we get a 2? We can either put a one on the zero die or a 2 on the one die. At this stage we have the situation in Figure 11.

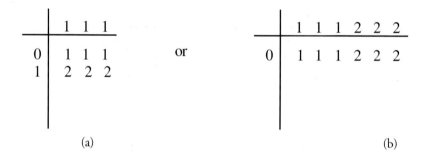

Figure 11

The combination of Figure 11 (a) now gives the option of either a 2 or three 3s to give a total of 3.

Further Explorations

33. In how many different ways can you finish off the dice in Figure 11(a)?

34. In how many ways can you finish off the dice in Figure 11(b)?

But our second option is to try 1, -, -, -, -, - and 0, 0, 0, -, -, -. To make a 2 we can have 1, 2, -, -, -, - and 0, 0, 0, -, -, - or 1, -, -, -, -, - and 0, 0, 0, 1, 1, 1. We explore this option in Figure 12.

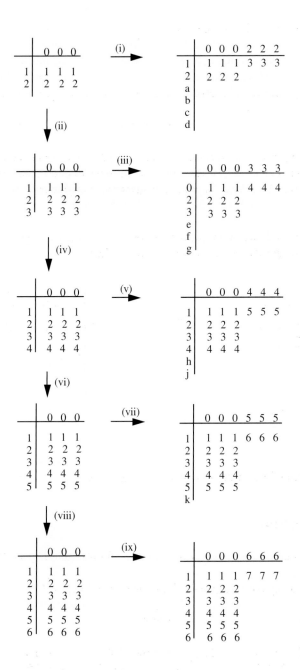

Figure 12

The plan of campaign in Figure 12 says that we can either (i) add 2s to one die or (ii) add a 3 to the other to get the three 3s. With (i) we can fill in three 4s in the second row when the one 2 adds to the three 2s. So from here we don't have much choice. You've got to get three 5s somewhere, so a is either 5 $(5 + 0 = 5)$ or 3 $(3 + 2 = 5)$. But 3 is no good because it gives three more 3s. Hence a is 5.

You then have to get 6, so $b = 6$. Then $c = 9$ and $d = 10$ follow fairly naturally. The route (i) then gives 0, 0, 0, 2, 2, 2 and 1, 2, 5, 6, 9, 10.

Going along path (ii) gives us the two options (iii) and (iv). Pathway (iii) really gives no room to manoeuvre. Three 5s and three 6s can be added straight away. Then we are more or less forced to get 0, 0, 0, 3, 3, 3 and 1, 2, 3, 7, 8, 9.

But (iv) leads on to (v) which requires h to be 9, otherwise we can't get three 9s without creating more 5s than we can handle. However, with $h = 9$ we get three 13s. So (v) is no good to us.

Now (vi) leads to (vii) which forces k to be 11 and we get no 12. And (viii) leads to the solution 0, 0, 0, 6, 6, 6 and 1, 2, 3, 4, 5, 6 in (ix).

The Figure 12 route gives us the first three pairs of dice in Figure 13. The fourth pair comes from 1, -, -, -, -, - and 0, 0, 0, 1, 1, 1. The other pairs of dice come from your work earlier, starting with 0, -, -, -, -, - and 1, 1, 1, -, -, -.

0, 0, 0, 2, 2, 2 and 1, 2, 5, 6, 9, 10 ;	0, 0, 0, 3, 3, 3 and 1, 2, 3, 7, 8, 9;
0, 0, 0, 6, 6, 6 and 1, 2, 3, 4, 5, 6 ;	0, 0, 0, 1, 1, 1 and 1, 3, 5, 7, 9, 11;
1, 1, 1, 2, 2, 2 and 0, 2, 4, 6, 8, 10 ;	1, 1, 1, 3, 3, 3 and 0, 1, 4, 5, 8, 9;
1, 1, 1, 4, 4, 4 and 0, 1, 2, 6, 7, 8 ;	1, 1, 1, 7, 7, 7 and 0, 1, 2, 3, 4, 5.

Figure 13

Further Explorations

35. Are you convinced there are only eight pairs of dice and they are shown in Figure 13?

36. Do the solutions of Figure 13 fall into classes in some way? Can you see any resemblance between pairs of solutions?

◆ ◆ ◆

Suppose we start with 0, 0, 0, 2, 2, 2 and 1, 2, 5, 6, 9, 10. We can get another solution by adding one to each number of the first die and subtracting one from each number of the second die. Or we can subtract one from the first die provided we add one to each number of the second die. Of course, this will mean that we'll get negative numbers on the dice but if we are prepared to do that, we can get the whole family of pairs of dice we see in Figure 14.

3,	3,	3,	5,	5,	5	and	-2,	-1,	2,	3,	6,	7
2,	2,	2,	4,	4,	4	and	-1,	0,	3,	4,	7,	8
1,	1,	1,	3,	3,	3	and	0,	1,	4,	5,	8,	9
0,	0,	0,	2,	2,	2	and	1,	2,	5,	6,	9,	10
-1,	-1,	-1,	1,	1,	1	and	2,	3,	6,	7,	10,	11
-2,	-2,	-2,	0,	0,	0	and	3,	4,	7,	8,	11,	12

Figure 14

Further Explorations

37. Figure 14 shows that two of the solutions of Figure 13 are in the same family. Are there any other Figure 13 solutions in the same family?

38. The family in Figure 14 could be described by a, a, a, a + 2, a + 2, a + 2 and −a + 1, −a + 2, −a + 5, −a + 6, −a + 9, −a + 10. Check that this general description does give the property that Snakeye wants.

39. Describe all the other families in a similar manner to that of the last Exploration.

40. The total of all the spots in the two dice of the family of solutions in Exploration 39 is, surprisingly, 39. Are the sums in Exploration 40, 40?

41. Can you explain the result you got in the last Exploration?

42. Does knowing the sums of the dots help to get the families more efficiently?

43. Generalise or extend the problem.

44. What heuristics have you used in this chapter? Bring your heuristics' file up to date.

45. Have a look at the list of difficulties that you made as the chapter progressed. Which of these have now been solved for you? How was this done? (Was it something we said? Did you work it out for yourself?)

Which difficulties have you not resolved? What would you need to know to be able to resolve them? (Maybe you should talk to a friend.)

4. CHAPTER SUMMARY

In this chapter we suggested the following strategies:

> be systematic;
> use a decision tree;
> use a diagram;
> use a table;
> use algebra;
> generalize and extend.

We also discussed what mathematicians do again and came to the conclusion that the process of mathematics is exactly the same as that of problem solving.

This chapter gave us a chance to look at another investigation. This was triggered by the desire to generalize or extend Snakeye's problem.

CHAPTER 8   THE FARMYARD

1. LEGS

Wandering round in the yard there are some ducks and some pet lambs. There are 13 creatures in all with a total of 40 legs. How many lambs are there?

We never really understand why anyone would be interested in such a question. After all, if you happened to be in the yard you could quickly count the lambs and if you weren't what nerd would have given you such obtuse information? A worm perhaps? Bear with us though, until we expose the answer.

So how can we solve the problem? If there were 2 lambs, there'd be 11 ducks and that would give 30 legs. So try 10 lambs and 3 ducks. No, 46 legs is too many. What next then?

Well, we could keep up this trial and error using the wildcatting approach. We presumably would eventually hit the right answer. However, already in Chapter 6 we poo-pooed this idea. Hitting or missing is not consistent with the best practice in mathematics (unless we have no other ideas). When we are in a problem solving situation what we have to do is to use strategies that will enable us to get the right answer, if possible, in the shortest possible time.

Problem solving is like pouring wine through a funnel into a bottle but not knowing at the outset which funnel to use, nor which bottle the wine has to end up in. In the analogy the funnel is the method of solution and the bottle the answer. We have the wine (the problem) and we must use our ingenuity to force it to reveal both the funnel and the bottle. In some way, both method and answer are tied up in the problem itself. There is no real hope trying to guess the answer, trying to guess ahead of time what bottle will eventually be used. For most problems there are too many possible answers. Surprisingly it's a little easier to look for funnels. This is because there are some general funnels that, with a little modification for the particular wine we're dealing with, can be used to good effect.

So let's go back to the animal problem. As we fairly strongly hinted now in both Chapter 6 and earlier here, trial and error without any system is just a list-and-hope strategy. Possibly useful to get a feel for the problem in hand but, unless we're very lucky, not likely to get us an answer.

The first useful funnel then, is being systematic and doing an exhaustive search.

Further Explorations

1. How can you do an exhaustive search in the legs' problem?

    How many calculations will need to be undertaken to complete the search?

    Is this a good strategy here?

2. Complete the exhaustive search. What conclusion did you reach?

3. What are the limitations of an exhaustive search?

While we think of it. Make a difficulties list again in this chapter. We'll ask you to analyse this list at the end.

Although trial and error is not a good funnel to use in general, it's close relative **trial and improve** is. The point of this strategy is to have an initial guess (trial) and use the result of that guess to have a better next guess.

To see this, let's look at the first guess we had at the start of the section. There we tried 2 lambs and 11 ducks. Unfortunately, 2 lambs and 11 ducks only have 30 legs between them, not 40. So how can we improve the 2 lambs guess? Well, we just use the observation that we need another 10 legs. Surely that means we increase the number of lambs, because lambs have more legs than ducks.

So let's try 5 lambs and 8 ducks. This little collection have 36 legs so we're getting close. We still need to increase the number of lambs though because 36 is still less than 40. What about 8 lambs and 5 ducks? 42 legs! We've gone too far. Will 7 lambs do the trick?

Further Explorations

4. Complete the trial and improve method.

5. In this problem you can improve the trial and improve funnel. You should actually be able to go from the 2 lamb guess to the correct answer in only one step. How?

6. Can trial and improve be used on the main questions of the last two chapters?

7. What assumptions does the trial and improve method make. Are those assumptions valid here?

8. What are the limitations of the trial and improve method?

Actually now might be a good time to try using a **table**. Tables often give us a better feeling for a problem than working out a lot of examples that we leave scattered all over the page. Gathering together numbers in a systematic way is often useful. So we've produced Table 1.

lambs	ducks	legs
0	13	26
1	12	28
2	11	30
3	10	32
4	9	34
5	8	36
6	7	38
7	6	40
8	5	42
9	4	44
10	3	46
11	2	48
12	1	50
13	0	52

Table 1

Well, the first thing that we notice about Table 1 is that we have actually carried out an exhaustive search and the unique answer is clearly 7 lambs. But, of course, we didn't have to do all this work. You could see from Table 1 that the number of legs was increasing by 2 each time we increased the number of lambs. We started off from 26 legs and we had to get to 40. So it should have been relatively easy to see we had to have 7 lambs.

Further Explorations

9. Can we justify (or prove) that the legs go up by 2 each time as we come down the table?

10. Why does starting at 26 legs mean we need 7 lambs to get 40 legs?

11. A total of 17 owls and pussycats went to sea in a beautiful pea green boat. Between them they had 46 legs. How many owls were there?

12. Make up your own problem on the same theme. Solve it. Justify your answer.

◆ ◆ ◆ ◆

Now we know that zero lambs (and 13 ducks) give us 26 legs. What's more, every time we add a lamb and remove a duck, we add on 4 − 2 = 2 legs. So for ducks we have

26 + lots of 2 legs.

The number of legs we're after is 40. The number represented by the empty square has to be 7.

Further Explorations

13. How many lambs would there be if we had a total of 46 legs? (Don't cheat by looking at Table 1. Use the ☐ approach.)

14. Solve Explorations 11 and 12 using the ☐ method.

15. What would be the answer if there were 49 legs?

◆ ◆ ◆ ◆

Now in Table 2 below, we know that the legs increase by 2 as we go down,

lambs	legs
0	26
1	28
2	30
3	32
4	34
.	.
.	.

Table 2

Can we find a rule here? The jumps are in twos. Zero lambs give us 26 legs; one lamb gives us 28 legs; two lambs give 30 legs, and so on. This means that we have the following rule:

$$\text{number of legs} = 26 + 2 \times (\text{numbers of lambs}).$$

Further Explorations

16. What is the legs' rule in Explorations 11 and 12?

17. How would you use the rule above to solve the original legs' problem?

But getting across from lambs to legs we can put in another column in Table 2 to give Table 3.

lambs	?	legs
0	+26	26
1	+27	28
2	+28	30
3	+29	32
4	+30	34

Table 3

What is the rule for the middle column? The number there is always 26 more than the number of lambs. So if we said there were L lambs, there would be L + 26 in the middle column.

But we get the number of legs by adding across the Table. Hence

$$\begin{aligned}\text{Number of legs} &= \text{number of lambs} + (L + 26) \\ &= L + (L + 26) \\ &= 2L + 26.\end{aligned}$$

Further Explorations

18. Use the last rule to show that for 40 legs we need 7 lambs.

19. Use the same method to solve the problems in Explorations 11, 12 and 13.

◆ ◆ ◆ ◆

Now some of you have met algebra. This is an enormous funnel that can be used on many problems. In the current animal problem, let L be the number of lambs and d the number of ducks. Now we know that there are 13 ducks. So L + d = 13.

On the other hand, we know something about the number of legs. Since every lamb contributes 4 legs, there must be 4L lamb's legs. And since every duck has 2 legs, there are 2d duck's legs. So 4L + 2d = 40.

We now have two equations in two unknowns, namely,

$$L + d = 13 \qquad .....(1)$$
$$4L + 2d = 40 \qquad .....(2)$$

For those of you who understand algebra, solving these two equations should be a snap.

Further Explorations

20. Solve equations (1) and (2).

21. Can the two problems of the last two chapters be solved by algebra?

22. Is algebra a universal funnel? In other words, can you solve every problem using algebra?

One thing we haven't done so far is to draw a diagram. So let's see if we can find the number of lambs using a pictorial method. In Figure 1, we've drawn 13 blobs to represent the animals. But how can we use these blobs?

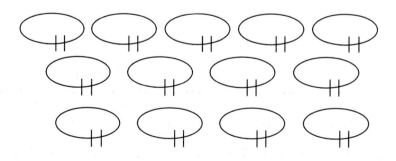

Figure 1

Every blob has at least two legs, so put two "legs" per blob as we did in Figure 1. All told, 26 legs have gone. That leaves 14. How will you finish the problem?

Further Explorations

23. Finish the diagrammatic approach to the problem.

24. Use a diagrammatic method to solve Explorations 11, 12 and 13.

25. Could you use concrete materials to solve the problem?

You are probably sick of legs of lamb by now but bear with us for just a little while longer.

Just imagine you have lined the 13 animals up in the yard. Tell them to stand on their two feet (their two back feet if there is a choice). Then tell them to raise their other feet in the air. All we have to do now is to count the feet that are waving around and divide by two. The number we get is the number of lambs.

Further Explorations

26. Use the "stand on your own two (back) feet" method to solve the animal problem.

27. Will the "stand on your own two feet" method work with any problem like the yard problem?

28. Is "standing on your own two feet" a funnel that can be used on any other problem?

29. Does this remind you of anything you've seen before? Does the name "Fiona" ring any bells?

The final thing that we want to say about problem solving in this section, is that it's all about taking the problem and forcing it into a corner. You have to manipulate what you're given so that it tells you the answer. But you have to use clever manipulation to do this. The harder the problem, the cleverer your manipulation will need to be.

The thing that's also worth noting is that almost every problem has a range of cleverness associated with it. Let's run through the methods of solution to the legs' problem to confirm this.

If you recall, there were several methods of solution. These were

(1)   trial and error;
(2)   exhaustive search;
(3)   trial and improve;
(4)   make a table;
(5)   algebra;
(6)   stand on your own feet;
(7)   use a diagram;
(8)   use concrete materials;
(9)   give up.

How did we use these methods to squeeze the answer out of the problem?

By itself, trial and error doesn't enable you to funnel the wine into the right bottle. Trial and error might give you some ideas as to what the problem is and where you might attack it but it won't force it into a corner.

In some cases trial and error can be adjusted to trial and improve. Using what information you know about the problem you may be able to make your next trial a better one than your last trial. That way you may hone in on the correct answer. So trial and improve does get you to the right bottle after first checking out a few other bottles.

In problems where all of the cases can be listed fairly simply, and systematically, then an exhaustive search is a possible strategy. What you're doing here is essentially trying all the bottles. The disadvantage of an exhaustive search is that it may take a long time. If you can program a computer to do this search for you, then it may not matter too much. However, even computers take time to do things. So if there are an enormous number of cases, even writing a program may not help.

One of the advantages of the exhaustive search strategy is that it tells you **everything** about **every** case of the problem. That's like knowing about **all** the bottles. This information might be useful later, for another problem. It will also be useful if, as in the case of the circle problem in Chapter 6, there is more than one possible answer. An exhaustive search will throw up such possibilities.

Actually if the problem has more than one answer, you may miss it if you are using a trial and improve approach. With trial and improve you tend to hone in on one answer. So any other possible answer may be missed.

One thing that is frequently useful in exhaustive searches is to draw up a table of values. The idea of the table is that it is a compact way of writing down all the data that you produce. But tables can be useful for the trial and improve technique or to help you come up with good conjectures in problems where that is appropriate. So, if in doubt, draw up a table. Tables do have the advantage of storing data efficiently. It's better to do things systematically in a table then have them scattered all over several pieces of paper. In addition, the first few values of a table sometimes illustrate a pattern which can be used to extend the list more quickly.

Algebra is a very powerful tool. In problems where it can be used it will inevitably work and work well. One of algebra's powers is that it will enable all answers to be found. It happens that there are problems that can be set up using algebra but the algebra alone is insufficient to produce an answer. This type of problem usually involves more unknowns than there are equations or involves equations which are not easy to solve. We'll look at some situations like this later. It's actually interesting to note that reasonably often, when you can set up a problem algebraically, it turns out that there is a quicker, neater, more efficient approach. While finding nice solutions is good, some of us are happy with any solution we can get. If you know algebra and can set up the problem in hand algebraically, go for it.

"Standing on your own feet" is a technique that worked with the legs' problem and the Mothers' Day card problem too. We mention it here because it is a nice neat, incisive, elegant method of solution. While algebra works efficiently with the legs' problem there is something more appealing about the "stand on your own feet" method. You could explain this very quickly to almost anyone. Your father is likely to have forgotten any algebra he ever knew but even he could cope with "standing on your own feet".

Many problems have a clever method of solution. These methods usually require a bit of lateral thinking or a lucky flash of inspiration when the penny drops. Sometimes these insights come after working on a problem for a while. Sometimes they come after you've found a solution by some other route. If you have some time in hand, it's worth spending it looking for the elegant method. This is part of what Pólya is on about in the "looking back" phase.

Using a diagram in the legs' problem turned out to be quite useful. In the end it happened to do for us what "standing on your own feet" did. If you remember, we also used diagrams to see where we were going with the dice problem of Chapter 7. Because some people seem to be better able to understand things by visualising them, diagrams are a good thing to try. Even if you are not a great visualiser, drawing a picture of some kind can be useful.

Now diagrams by themselves, do not usually provide cast iron proofs. Generally some words are needed to make sure that your idea is correct. However, diagrams are great for getting ideas and seeing relationships. Whenever you are lost for an idea, try drawing a diagram.

Concrete materials or equipment can act in a similar way to diagrams. They are good for getting ideas but they have the drawback that, if a proof is needed, then words need to be added to the inspiration the concrete materials gave. Incidentally, concrete materials are particularly good for primary age children and for those of us who find it easier to think with something "on the table" rather than abstractly in our heads.

And finally there's giving up. Fortunately we haven't had to do this yet. (But then, we're choosing the problems so we wouldn't expect to have to give up.) Problems vary in difficulty and what is difficult for us maybe easy for you. Don't worry about giving up on a problem for awhile. As we have already said, when you think you have stopped work on a problem your brain may still be ticking over. So take a break, read the paper, watch TV, go to the loo, whatever, you may find that, just when you were thinking about something completely different, a great idea suddenly pops into your head.

Further Explorations

In this set of explorations we want you to look at the problems and write down which of the eight methods we listed above, you would use to solve the problem. Try one of these approaches until you get a correct solution. Then see if one of the other methods will work too. If you come up with some completely different technique, then note that as well.

30. In the room there are spiders and flies - 21 in all. There are also 128 legs. How many spiders are there?

31. Can the numbers 1, 2, 3, 4, 5, 6, 7, 8 be placed, one in each of the unshaded squares, so that the sum of the three numbers on each side of the larger square is the same? (If the answer to this question is yes, find out in how many ways this can be done.)

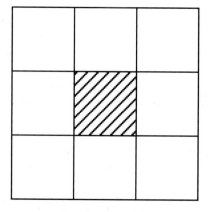

32. I was 24 years old when my daughter was born. How old will she be when I am twice as old as she is?

33. Sarah was 27 years old when she bought her new puppy, Lucy. How old will Sarah be when she is four times as old as Lucy?

2. SOME BIG WORDS

In Chapter 7, we tried to introduce you to the BIG problem solving picture. There we repeated the "mathematics" diagram which linked the problem to the experimenting to the conjecture to the proof to the solution and then, maybe, to a generalisation or extension. For some problems this diagram is a little complicated. Sometimes the experimenting leads directly to a method of solution, a funnel, and there's no need for a conjecture which you then set out to prove.

In the legs' problem, for instance, there was no need to make a conjecture. It wasn't a very complicated problem so when we forced it into a corner it revealed its answer quite quickly. We didn't need to force it first to a stage where we guessed we had the answer (the conjecture stage), and before we could find a proof.

These rag tag and bob tail tricks we already know are called **heuristics** (see p. 12). Heuristics are not infallible techniques. Rather they are things that might work now on this problem and almost certainly will work sometime on some problem you come across, maybe tomorrow. So heuristics are things you try in the hope that they will lead you to a solution. They hopefully, serve to discover.

There are an enormous number of heuristics. As we go through this book we'll announce when we've introduced another one. Almost certainly you introduced a new heuristic for yourself when you tackled the last set of exercises. They were meant to be reminiscent of other problems earlier in the book. You therefore might have used the "have I seen anything like this before?" heuristic. Some of the methods that you've seen elsewhere, can be advantageous for use in your current problem. So it's worth thinking back, if you are stuck for an idea, to something you may have seen or done before. In fact we suggest that this is the first thing you think when you see a problem for the first time.

Naturally the more heuristics that you have at your fingertips the better you will be at problem solving. Whenever you get stuck with a problem, cast your eye over your heuristics' file in the hope that it will provide you with some inspiration.

The other big word we wanted to get off our chests is **metacognition**. This simply means "thinking about your thinking". We've actually talked a lot so far about the way problem solving works and what we're looking for and where we are going. All this is part of metacognition. It helps you to keep control over what you are doing. It suggests to you which of a range of options might be worth taking at any stage. It essentially is what the decision tree is all about.

In addition to helping to decide what method to try, metacognition should also tell you that you've tried this method for too long and it's time to try something else. So look for another heuristic. If you find an answer of 5 cm to a problem involving the height of a mountain, metacognition should tell you there's something fishy. When you are stuck, metacognition will check to see if you have made an error or if there is a piece of information in the problem that you have so far avoided or if there is an unjustified assumption that you are making.

Metacognition also has its affective domain. Beliefs which you have, which may well be unjustifiable, may stop you from starting a problem or finishing too early. For instance, you may decide, on the basis of intuition only, that this problem has no solution and so you won't even make a start on it. Or you may believe that if a problem can't be solved in two minutes, it can't be solved at all. Some of us think that we can't do geometry problems. All of these beliefs show metacognition at work.

Schoenfeld is one researcher who has done a lot of work on metacognition. He concludes that the better the metacognition the better the problem solver. So monitoring or controlling your thoughts while you are working on a problem, is very important. It's a skill that we will try to help you achieve as you go through this book.

Further Explorations

34. Bring your heuristics' file up to date.

35. Have a look at the difficulties list that you compiled for this chapter. Which of these difficulties have been resolved and which haven't?

    Did resolving some of the difficulties from the last chapter help you with this chapter at all?

3. CHAPTER SUMMARY

In this chapter we used the following strategies:

> trial and error (guess and check);
> trial and improve (guess and improve);
> exhaustive search;
> make a table;
> use algebra;
> use a diagram;
> use concrete materials (equipment);
> stand on your own feet.

The word **metacognition**, thinking about your thinking, was introduced to make us realise that problem solving requires us to carefully monitor out thought processes.

CHAPTER 9   CASE STUDIES

1. WHAT ARE CASE STUDIES?

In this chapter we will look at several problems. We will solve them, with our usual amount of chat, on the left hand side of the page. Because problem solving causes the brain to be overactive and, hopefully, to have lots of good ideas, we put some of these good ideas on the right hand side of the page, opposite the point on the left hand side where we had the good idea.   Comments or questions also go on the right hand side.   In fact, anything of a metacognitive nature goes there.   In this context, a case study is like thinking out loud and trying to give some idea of why certain decisions were made.

The point of these case studies is really what is happening on the right hand side of the page.   In this chapter we want to hone up your metacognitive skills for you.   As you read the case studies, solution and the metacognition, note your own metacognition.   What questions are you asking yourself?   What heuristics can you see that we have missed?   Why did we put that comment in, and so on?

Finally, it's worth noting that the problems we are talking about here are not easy.   We don't necessarily expect you to be able to do them on you own.   Try to see how we do them though.   What general steps do we take and how do they help?

2. THE 13-PUZZLE*

The first problem is

Can the numbers 1, 2, 3, 4, 5, 6, 7, 8, 9 be placed, one per square in the diagram below, so that the sum of the numbers in any three consecutive horizontal or vertical squares is 13?

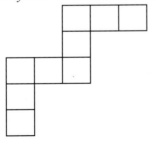

* We would like to express our thanks to Coralie Daniels for her thoughts on this problem, and for her willingness to have them used in this chapter. Some of the interesting solutions arose during her research for *Identification of Mathematical Ability and of Factors Significant in its Nurture* (in preparation) and were presented in *Different Approaches to Problem*

Solving, a paper presented at the HPM Conference held in Cairns, 1995.

Step 1: The Start: First of all, let's make sure that we understand the problem. We can only use the 9 digits in the given squares. We can only use one digit per square. The numbers in each of the two horizontal bits have to **add** up to **13** and so do the three numbers in each of the vertical bits.

One thing we can deduce straight away is that exactly one number goes in each square. It's also worth noting the fact that the numbers 1 through 9 are to be used is important. And "add up to 13" gives two more key pieces of information.

Are the squares important? Would it matter if they were circles as long as they were in the same relative positions as the squares. So the configuration of circles below ought to give the same result as the original problem.

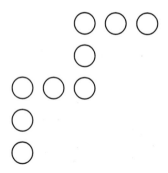

That means that we are unlikely to need to know anything about the properties of squares in order to do this problem.

What does the problem ask? What are we given? Which of the pieces of data in the problem are important? Can we state the problem in our own words?

If any of the pieces of information are changed we get a different problem. Using only some of the digits is not allowed. Repeating a digit is not on either. Adding up to 13 in some places and to 14 or something else, elsewhere, is wrong too.

All this initial stuff is about **understanding the problem**. Remember "Read the problem, Heed the problem."

It's the three in a row or three vertical that's important. Not the shape of the boxes we put the numbers in.

Step 2. Getting Started. Can we remember techniques we've tried before? We were rude about trial and error but we might just fluke it so let's try that one first. If nothing else, we might get some idea about other ways of tackling the problem if we do. So let's throw in a few digits and see what we get. Or maybe we should try a systematic search. After all there can't be too may cases to try. Ah no! Trial and error is easier. You don't have to think so hard.

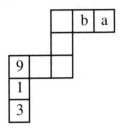

Let's throw in the 9 somewhere. We start with the 9 simply because we have to start somewhere and 9 is the biggest number. So if we're to be systematic, it's a good idea to start with 9. We're not sure where it goes. It's position might actually be a key to the problem. So put it in an "elbows" square where it can dominate a horizontal and a vertical bit. Once we've done that, we have to have a 1 and a 3 in either the vertical or horizontal section.

Now that's interesting. We could put the 1 above the 3 or the 3 above the 1. There's a bit of latitude there. And we're going to find the same thing on the horizontal bit dangling off to the right. The order of the numbers on the squares marked a and b is irrelevant to the final answer, if there is one.

It's heuristics time. "Choose a strategy." How can we tackle this problem? What has worked before?

- have we seen anything like this before?
- trial and error
- exhaustive search
- trial and improve
- algebra
- stand on your own feet
- use a diagram
- be systematic
- give up

Here's a crunch time. We've got two competing ideas (trial and error and systematic search). Which is the better? A sophisticated problem solver might try the exhaustive search first. However, a bit of trial and error is always appealing. Why don't we try the systematic search?

How can we get 13 using a 9?

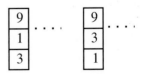

Both arrangements equally valid.

Hmmm. One of the things that this tells us is that if there is **one** answer then there will have to be **four**. If we get one answer we can get another by interchanging 1 and 3; and other by interchanging a and b and leaving 1 and 3; another by interchanging 1 and 3, **and** a and b.

This tells us something about the nature of any answer.

So let's keep going with the "9 in the elbow" trial. What else makes 13 with 9? We need two numbers that add together to make 4. Hang on! This can only be done using 1 and 3. Of course 2 + 2 would work but then we'd be using 2 twice. Some other number would have to be missed.

Trial and error is starting to tell us something. There is only one way to get 13 using a 9.

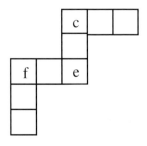

OK. So we can only make 13 with 9 by adding 1 and 3. Hence 9 can't be in an elbow square. We'll have to keep 9 away from squares c, e and f. Does something similar happen with 8? Now 8 + 4 + 1 = 13, 8 + 3 + 2 = 13 and these are the only ways to get 13. Oh, but that's not as useful as the 9 case. Because 8 can be used in two sums, then 8 could be in one of the elbow squares.

Note the systematic way we constructed 13 starting from 8. We tried 4 first and then 3, working down from largest to smallest. If we tried 8 + 2 + ?, this ? would have to be 3, which is higher than 2, so we must have done that case already.

Ah! But this has sparked off an idea. What if we listed all ways of getting 13 and see how they fit together?

Step 3: All 13 sums approach. So how can we list all the possible ways of getting 13 using three distinct digits? When we worked with 8 we got the two possibilities working systematically. How can we work systematically to find all sums?

Trial and error has told us to look for all the ways of getting 13. That might speed up the trial and error process. It'll cut out some alternatives.

The idea is again, to be systematic. But how?

We started off before working with 9 and then 8. Let's start from the top for the first number of the three and work down. Then start as high as we can for the second number and work down.

9 + 3 + 1 = 13.
8 + 4 + 1 = 13.
8 + 3 + 2 = 13.
7 + 5 + 1 = 13.
7 + 4 + 2 = 13.
7 + 3 + 3 = 13. Forget this.
6 + 6 + 1 = 13. This too.
6 + 5 + 2 = 13.
6 + 4 + 3 = 13.
5 + 7 + 1 = 13. We've already got these
5 + 6 + 2 = 13. two.
5 + 5 + 3 = 13 Can't have two 5's.
5 + 4 + 4 = 13 Two fours!!
4 + 8 + 1 = 13 Been there!
4 + 7 + 2 = 13 Done that!
4 + 6 + 3 = 13 No!
4 + 5 + 4 = 13 No!

We have had these first three already.

As we did earlier with 8, let the second number be 4 and then 3 and so on downwards until you can't go any further.

Actually we suspect we ought to be able to be more systematic than this. Let's come back to this later.

It's beginning to look as if we've got them all. Surely if we start with a 3 we would have to use numbers bigger than 3 to get 13?

So it looks as if the only sums we can have are:

9 + 3 + 1 = 13
8 + 4 + 1 = 13.
8 + 3 + 2 = 13.
7 + 5 + 1 = 13.
7 + 4 + 2 = 13.
6 + 5 + 2 = 13.
6 + 4 + 3 = 13.

Until we've shown this step conclusively we may miss an answer. Can you be sure we don't have to worry about a 1, 2, or 3 at the start?

There only seem to be seven sums.

If you look back at the squares you'll see there'll have to be **four** sums in any answer. Would it help if we could see which sums aren't going to work?

After a bit of trial and error we seem to have adopted a method where we systematically put 13 sums into the configuration of squares.

What have we got to go on? All we seem to know is that the 9 + 3 + 1 sum has to be used somewhere. It's the only sum with 9 in it. On the other hand, all the other digits occur in at least two sums so anything but 9 is an elbow candidate.

Which sums won't work? Are there some obvious "bad" sums?

Suppose we tried the 9 + 3 + 1 arrangement below. What have we got

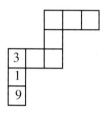

left? Only four possible sums. Ah ha! But two of these sums have a 3. If we use one we can't use the other. But if we don't use 8 + 3 + 2 here we won't be able to use 8 at all. And note that 8 can't now be in an elbow square. This is because we only have one sum with an 8 left in the four above. This gives us:

Using 9 + 3 + 1 means we can now only use the following sums from our seven possibilities; 9 and 1 have been used already:

8 + 3 + 2 (in the row with 3)
7 + 4 + 2
6 + 5 + 2
6 + 4 + 3 (in the row with 3)

Where can the 8 go?

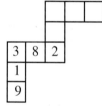

We have still to use two 13 sums. We only have two sums left. But both contain 2. So we can't finish off the situation with 3 in an elbow position. Better put 1 there and see what happens.

What sums are now left?
7 + 4 + 2
6 + 5 + 2

We can't use 6 + 4 + 3 since the 3 has already been used.

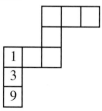

We see there are four possible sums left. If we used the 8 + 4 + 1, then the 8 couldn't be an elbow number because we only have one 13 sum with an 8 in. Let's try it.

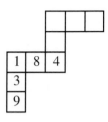

Obviously we have to now use the 7 + 4 + 2 sum. It's the only one with a 4 in it. And since 7 is in only one sum, it can't be the last elbow number. This gives us:

Putting 6 and 5 in any order give us an answer!

Step 4: Reflection. It's nice to have an answer. But have we solved the problem? Yes. We have surely? It asked "Can the numbers ....?" And we've shown they can. We're totally justified in quitting at this point. Go and get a cup of coffee if you want. Have a break.

Would you really be happy to quit now? Don't answer that! You know you'd never forgive yourself. You don't know if there are any other answers. You don't know if there is a better way of solving the problem.

What sums are available this time?

    8 + 4 + 1
    7 + 5 + 1
    7 + 4 + 2
    6 + 5 + 2

What sums are left now?

    7 + 4 + 2
    6 + 5 + 2

We've got an answer. Should we stop? Let's go to "Then look back".

Check the original problem. What did it say?

Is that all there is?

You would certainly be justified if you quit at this point. We'll go for just a bit longer.

Step 5: Is the answer unique? The obvious answer to that is "no". Having got one answer, we've actually got four! We talked about that earlier. Remember about interchanging a and b and so on. So we have four answers. But there's a sense in which those four answers are really the same. Surely fiddling a bit at the edges doesn't really give us anything new. If we thought of them as being somehow equivalent, then we only have one answer. Are there other answers not equivalent to the ones we've produced so far?

How did we get the answer above? What did we start out with? It was the $9 + 3 + 1$ sum. Can that sum go in another position?

Now we said that 9 wasn't an elbow number. So try it in the position in the diagram.

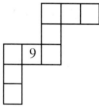

Should 1 go in the elbow on the left or on the right? Try the left first and see if that works.

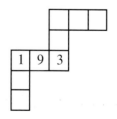

		2	5	6
		7		
1	8	4		
3				
9				

		2	6	5
		7		
1	8	4		
3				
9				

		2	5	6
		7		
1	8	4		
9				
3				

		2	6	5
		7		
1	8	4		
9				
3				

The four answers so far.

Search for another answer.

What sums are left from our original seven?

$$8 + 4 + 1$$
$$8 + 3 + 2$$
$$7 + 5 + 1$$
$$7 + 4 + 2$$
$$6 + 5 + 2$$
$$6 + 4 + 3$$

Actually that doesn't really get rid of too many other sums. On the left vertical section we could put either 8 + 4 + 1 or 7 + 5 + 1. Try them both.

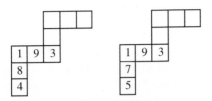

What sums are available now?

6 + 5 + 2   :   8 + 3 + 2
              :   6 + 4 + 3

Can we go any further?

The left one stops dead. We've got one sum left and we need two sums to complete this figure.

The right one doesn't work either. Whichever of the two sums we use next, in whichever order, we can't finish off the diagram with the other sum.

Perhaps 1 should have been in the right elbow. The 3 forces the two possibilities below.

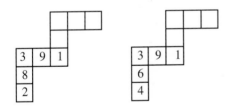

What sums are able to be used now?

7 + 5 + 1   :   7 + 5 + 1

That's a stopper!

So both of these are dead ends.

Well, it looks as if 9 will have to go round the bend a bit.

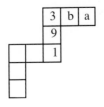

Haven't we seen something like this before though?

Hang on! If we tried to fill in the a, b squares and then the rest, and if we were successful, then we could have finished off the last case with $3 + 9 + 1$ in the lower horizontal bit. And we can use a similar argument if we swap the 1 and the 3 in the last diagram.

Use previous information plus symmetry to cut down your work.

And, similarly, it's no good putting 9 in the b square either. Well, maybe it is. If we put 9 in the b square we'd get the answer below.

It looks as if symmetry can help us cut down the number of possibilities, as well as saving us a lot of time working out things that are somehow just duplications.

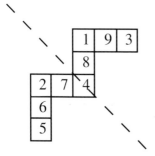

There is symmetry about a main diagonal.

Is that really a new answer? Swinging about the dotted diagonal gives us an answer we've already had. So is there really essentially one answer with seven other "equivalent" answers?

When is an answer not an answer?

We've now established all the possible answers.

One or eight, whatever, there aren't any other answers.

Step 6: A better way? How could there be a better way to solve this problem? Why should we bother anyway?

Let's keep looking back over what we've done. A philosophical question - or is it? A nifty answer here may lead us to better, quicker solutions somewhere else later.

That's actually a very good question that we'll duck at this point while we search for **another** (if not necessarily **better**) method of solution. Is it possible to come up with another solution out of the blue? Possibly not, so try to model a method for this problem on a similar problem that we've already done. Didn't the circles problem (see Chapter 6), have the same flavour as this problem? What proved worthwhile there?

Have you seen a problem like this before? Is there an old strategy that might come in handy at this point?

We seemed to get a fairly neat method in the circle problem by noting that

$$\begin{array}{ccc} \text{three times the sum of} & = & \text{sum of numbers} \\ \text{a side} & & 1 \text{ to } 6 \\ & & + \\ & & \text{sum of corner} \\ & & \text{numbers.} \end{array}$$

What is equivalent to this in the 13-puzzle? Or is there a similar idea.

Will something like that work with the 13-puzzle?

Can we find something similar for the sum of the horizontal and vertical bits? That sum is just the sum of the numbers from 1 to 9 surely?

The horizontal and vertical bits give $13 + 13 + 13 + 13 = 52$. The sum of the numbers from 1 to 9 is $1 + 2 + 3 + 4 + 5 + 6 + 7 + 8 + 9 = 45$. There's a discrepancy of 7. How come? What have we missed?

Can you find a quick way of adding the numbers from 1 to 9?

Ah! The corner, elbow squares! In the $13 + 13 + 13 + 13$, the elbow squares were counted twice!

It looks as if we may have found the equivalent bit we were looking for.

So 13 + 13 + 13 + 13 = 1 + 2 + 3 + 4 + 5 +
6 + 7 + 8 + 9 + the elbow squares.

The sum of the elbow squares is therefore 7.

An important revelation if ever there was one!

There are three elbow squares. How can three numbers from 1 to 9 add to 7?

$$6 + 1 + 0 = 7$$

Yes but 0 isn't a number from 1 to 9. The smallest numbers we can start with are 1 and 2. Now

$$1 + 2 + 4 = 7.$$

What about 1 and 3?

$$1 + 3 + 3 = 7$$

Can't use 3 twice, sorry.

Are you satisfied with this? The elbow squares have to add to 7 and there's only one way to do that. So the elbow numbers have to be 1, 2 and 4.

So it looks like only 1 + 2 + 4 satisfies the condition of three numbers adding to 7. Ah, so 1, 2, 4 are the elbow numbers!

How may ways are there to put 1, 2, 4 into the elbows?

But, to within symmetry, it seems there are three ways to put them into the 13- puzzle diagram. We've listed them below.

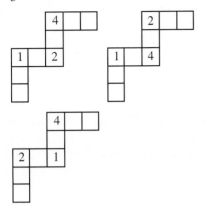

Now we know that only one of these configurations leads to an answer. Why do the other methods not work?

Ah that's easy! The other two methods have 1 and 2 in the same row. To take that row sum to 13 we'd need a 10! So we have to have:

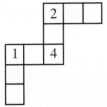

Once we've got this far, it's all down hill. The row with 1 and 4 in has to be completed by an 8. The column with 2 and 4 has to be completed by a 7.

Where does 9 go? It can't go with the 2. That could require 9 + 2 + 2 = 13. So it goes with the 1. The 3, 5 and 6 are then forced into position.

Hmm. That certainly was quicker than the first method.

This symmetry business looks useful.

Are you convinced that any other way of putting in 1, 2, 4 in the elbow squares, is equivalent to one of these? It's all to do with symmetry about that main diagonal.

Is there a good reason why only one of these configurations works?

Here's the advantage of seeking another method of solution. And we've found a "nice" "elegant" method. (Or would any method have been nice and elegant after that first way?)

Further Explorations

1. Are you sure that we don't have any sums making 13 like $3 + * + *$ where 3 is the largest of the three numbers?

2. (a) How many different ways are there of using four distinct whole numbers to give a sum of 13?

    (b) Repeat (a), replacing 13 by 24.

3. Does the 13-puzzle have one answer or 8 answers? What do you think and why?

4. Can one method of solution to a problem be better than another one? Look at the problems we've solved so far. Consider their methods of solution. Is any one method "better" than any other? Why?

5. Find a quick way of adding $1 + 2 + 3 + 4 + 5 + 6 + 7 + 7 + 9$. Use this approach to add the first 100 numbers. What has this got to do with Carl Friedrick Gauss?

    What other lots of numbers can be added quickly this way?

6. Convince yourself (and at least one friend) that there is only one way that three different numbers from 1 to 9 can add to 7.

7. Prove that there are only 3 inequivalent ways of filling the elbow squares with 1, 2 and 4.

8. Step 7: Extend the problem. If 13 is replaced by some other number, can the diagram be completed? Can you find all such numbers? (Does this remind you of Indy Anna-Jones?)

9. What questions or comments would you have added to the right hand side of the page.

10. What heuristics were used in this problem? Bring your heuristics' file up to date.

11. Can you find another way of doing this problem.

12. (a) Find all possible ways (to within equivalence) of putting the numbers 1, 2, 3, 4, 5, 6, 7, 8 into the arrangement of squares below so that the sum of any side of the larger square is 13.

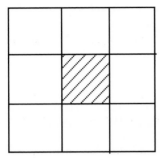

(The centre square is not to be used)

(b) Repeat (a) with 13 replaced by some other number. Which "other numbers" produce no answers? Why?

13. (a) A magic square is one in which all rows, columns and the two major diagonals sum to the same numbers. Use the numbers 1 to 9 to produce a magic square in the figure below.

a	b	c
d	e	f
g	h	i

(Remember when you're finished, $a + d + g = b + e + h = c + f + i = a + b + c = d + e + f = g + h + i = a + e + i = c + e + g$.)

(b) Find all such magic squares.

(c) Can you find a more elegant way of doing this?

(d) What nine different numbers can be used to form a magic square? (Remember the Temple of Gloom.)

14. What metacognition did you see?

15. What scaffolding would have been a help?

3. Handshakes

After a particularly enjoyable game, each team shook hands with everyone on the other team. The person in charge of the game shook hands with members of both teams. There were 255 handshakes altogether. What game had they been playing?

Step 1. The Start. What on earth has the question got to do with a game? We haven't got a clue about that so we'll ignore it for the moment and hope for inspiration. We suppose it might be possible to find out the number of players on each team.

Understand the problem.
Don't worry if we're panicking. It's all part of the process. Have confidence that you can solve the problem. Hang in there.

But what are the key points in the problem? On the two teams, everyone shook hands with everyone else. The umpire or ref or whoever, shook hands with both teams. Our guess is that if we change anything there we'll get a different question. And surely the number 255 is no accident. If it was only 3 then we'd be in quite a different ball game. (We suppose the teams were playing a ball game?)

What are the key items in the problem?

Presumably each team has the same number of players.

So there's this game where all the players shake hands and the ref, or whoever, shakes hands with all the players. There are 255 handshakes and we've got to find out what the game is.

Reword the problem to help you to understand it.

Step 2. Getting started. There's no way that we can solve this problem straight away. We're going to need to work up to it. If we try a few special cases we might get a better idea of what's going on.

The question's too hard. Can we scale it down?
Adopt the strategy of trying a special case.

If it was a tennis doubles match, then our team would shake hands twice each with the opposition. That would make four handshakes. Then the umpire would shake hands with us all to give another four handshakes. That's a total of eight.

So it wasn't tennis. We suppose that was obvious. In tennis can you reach up high enough to shake hands with the umpire? An we would have shaken hands with our partners before we shook hands with the opposition.

Extra information being brought to bear.

This extra information is sometimes useful. Not everything is necessarily stated in the problem.
Is it important that people on the same team didn't shake hands with each other?

It's not clear to us how we're going to keep touch with all of these handshakes as the teams get larger. We won't be able to keep all the information in our head. At the moment we're just guessing. Unless we record the data we're not going to be able to improve our guess sensibly.

Looking for a strategy to record the data.

How about building up a table? We suppose we want to know the number of handshakes for the size of a team. When we fluke 255, we'll just read back to find the size of the team.

Use a table. But what should the entries be? Size of team and number of handshakes? Anything else?

Actually that's fine but it's not the direction we were heading. Even finding the number of handshakes when the team size is relatively large is not going to be easy. How are we going to keep track of them all with even three players on a team?

Some system is going to be needed to find the number of handshakes even if we know the number in the team.
Is it worth writing out a list of heuristics at this stage to get some inspiration?

Now we could act it out but we might not be able to find enough people to make up the teams. Will a diagram help? With two-person teams we could put a figure for each of the players and the ref.

Act it out?

team 1

team 2

"ref"

Draw a diagram?

But how can we represent the handshakes? Join two people if they shake hands? That sounds

Simplify the notation/diagram.

good. Hang on though, it's going to be a pain drawing all those figures for teams with 10 (if we get that far). Why don't we just put a dot for each person? Then we'll get this drawing for the two person team.

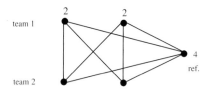

team 1

team 2

The total number of handshakes here is 2 + 2 + 4.

The numbers count the handshakes. The 2s count the handshakes between the teams and the 4 the handshakes with the referee. We don't need numbers on the second team's dots because their handshakes have all been counted on first team's dots.

Maybe we need to play around with this for a while. That sounds like experimenting.

Step 3. Experiment. The problem has been set up in Step 2 so all we have to do now is experiment and look for a pattern. We'll do teams of 3, 4, 5 and 6.

Hopefully we won't take long to rack up 255 handshakes.

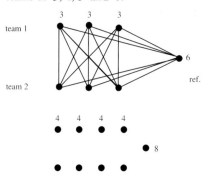

team 1

team 2

Number of handshakes?
3 + 3 + 3 + 6 = 15.

A further simplification of notation.

Now we know what's happening we don't need to put everything in.

It's easy enough to add up those numbers.

6 6 6 6 6 6
● ● ● ● ● ●

● 12

● ● ● ● ● ●

$36 + 12 \neq 255$ yet.

So the table so far looks like this

size of team	no. handshakes
2	8
3	15
4	24
5	35
6	48

Step 4 What next? It looks as if it's quite a large team. There's a long way from 48 to 255. But maybe it's worth guessing some sizes of teams to see what's happening. For instance, a netball team has 7 players, a hockey team 11 players, a League team 13, Rugby has 15, Australian Rules 18. Let's hope it's not a gridiron team including offence and defence plus reserves.

guess: 11

11 11 + 22 = 143 handshakes.
So the team is bigger than 11.

guess: 18

18 18 ... 18
● ● ... ●

● 36

● ● ... ●

18 18 + 36 = 360 handshakes.

Guess and Improve? Look for a pattern? What?

Try an exhaustive search. There are a range of strategies at this point. Which one you choose will probably depend on your faith in your own mathematical ability.

With guess and improve you can use the extra knowledge again.

So it's smaller than 18. It was actually never going to be Aussie Rules. They have more than one referee.

Looks like 15 might be a good bet.

guess: 15

15x15 + 30 = 255! Hooray.

So it's almost certainly a game of rugby. We can't think of any other game with 15 a side.

Step 5. Reflect. Was that the best way to do the problem? How else could I have done it?

Wait a minute. Maybe there's some other size team that gets 255 handshakes! How are we going to check that out?

Intuitively that's easy isn't it? Surely that's easy isn't it? Surely as the size of the team increases, so must the number of handshakes. But how to convince the cat of that?

Hang on. The diagram will do it for us. The two person team diagram is sitting inside the three person team diagram.

We'll leave you to explore these options soon.

Could there be two answers here. Remember with guess and check you may not necessarily hit **all** the answers.

Is there a way of showing that there can only be **one** way of getting 255?

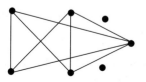

So we can get the diagram for any sized team by starting the step before and adding **extra** hand-shakes.

If the numbers go up each time, then 255 can only be found **once**. Beauty!

But what if there's a team of 101? How many handshakes would they produce? Heck. That wasn't what the question asked. I'll leave that for someone else to worry about.

The beginning of a generalisation.

Further Explorations

16. (a) What heuristics did you see being used in this case study?

    (b) What further heuristics would you have used if you had been doing the problem.
       (You may want to go through the problem again and think about this as you go.)

    (c) Bring your heuristics' file up to date.

17. (a) What evidence of metacognition did you see?

    (b) What evidence of metacognition was occurring in your own mind as you read through the problem?

    (c) What help would you have given the person tackling that problem in order to facilitate the solution? (We're talking scaffolding here.)

18. How many times was extra information used that wasn't contained in the original problem as it was posed?

19. Rephrase the problem in your own words.

20. At the beginning of Step 4 a number of heuristics are suggested. Would you use an exhaustive search in the problem? Why or why not?

21. What is the pattern here? Can you describe a rule for getting from the size of the team to the number of handshakes? Can you justify this rule?

22. If two teams with 101 players met, how many handshakes would there be?

23. The last two Explorations involve generalizations. Here's an extension.

    At a certain party everyone shook hands with everyone else. Someone recorded all these handshakes. There were 5356. How many people were there at the party?

24. Completely solve Exploration 23. What we mean by this is find a formula for the number of handshakes in terms of the number of people.

    Justify your answer. Convince two people that your justification is true.

25. Find another problem which has the same answer as the last Exploration.

26. Invent a problem which is similar to both the handshake problems in this section.

27. How would you use this problem with a class of primary school students?

    What would you hope they got out of such a problem?

28. Cover up the right hand side of the pages of the next section and add your own annotations. Then reveal the right hand side. Did you have many comments in common with ours? Is it so surprising if you don't?

4. FROGS

This is a game. The object is to get the black frogs from the right end of the board of squares, to the left end, and to get the white frogs from the left to the right. Frogs can move by going in to a vacant square next to them or by jumping over another frog. Can it be done? If it can, what's the fewest moves needed? Oh, black moves first.

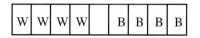

Step 1. We think we understand the problem. we've got to get the frogs to this position.

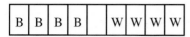

We can move frogs by "sliding" or by "jumping".

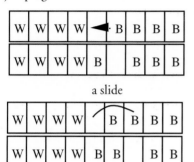

a slide

a jump

Before we go any further we're going to draw a lot of boards up so that we don't stop our flow of thought by having to draw boards all the time. No, Wait a minute! We'll draw up one board and use coloured counters to represent the frogs!

Heck! This can't be done! If we use slides, we can move all the blacks to the left and the whole thing comes to a halt, unless we start moving frogs back again and that doesn't seem a good idea.

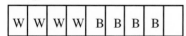

On the other hand, if we only use jumps we get in to the same pickle. The only advantage we can see is that with jumps we can get stuck in only two moves! (That's an advantage?)

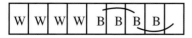

What are the key pieces of information in the problem?
Note that we have already used a notation.

Restate the problem in your own words.

Introduce terminology to reduce verbosity and help understanding and explanation.

Draw a diagram (lots!)
Use concrete materials.
If you've got some frogs handy use them.

What to do now? Where did we go wrong? Or maybe this just helps us know what not to do. It certainly looks bad having two or more black frogs together. Are there any other bad situations?

So it looks as if we'll need to work black and white interchangeably in some way. There are an awful lot of possible moves with four frogs on each side though.

It may be time to cut things down a bit. Why don't we try a smaller example?

Step 2. Small Example 1. We've called this small example 1 because we're almost certain that we're going to have to do more than one example before we see how to do the four frog problem.

OK then. One frog on each side. At least it's easier to draw the board!

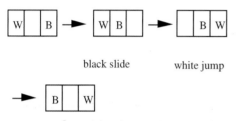

black slide   white jump

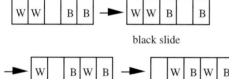

black slide

Well, that wasn't too hard. The one frog game can be done in 3 moves. Roll on Step 2.

It's nice to be able to do something even if it's a fairly small case.

Step 3. Small Example 2. Let's have a go at the two frogs a side.

There ought to be more meat in two frogs!

For the second move, we could do a black slide or a white jump. But we've already seen the problems of just moving blacks. So we white- jumped.

If we slid the black forward on the second move, we could do a white jump but then we'll have hemmed in two whites and a black on the right hand side.

The only alternative, if we're to keep the blacks going left and the whites going right, is to slide the white forward.

Now we're there. Two black jumps, a white slide a white jump and a black slide should do it. Here. We'll show you.

After a little experimentation it looks as if it's best to avoid having two frogs of the same colour next to each other until the very end.

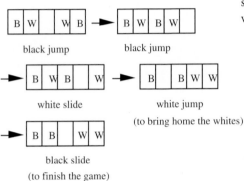

black jump   black jump

white slide   white jump

(to bring home the whites)

black slide

(to finish the game)

On a countback we did that in eight moves. We'd better check that we did it right. We were moving fast at the end.

It's tempting to look for a pattern already. You could start by drawing up a table of values.

Step 4. We feel strong enough to take on four frogs now. Now. Hang on. That's not such a cinch after all. We're sure we can do three frogs though. Yep! Just 15 moves and they're home in bed.

See what confidence you get from doing a couple of "easy" cases?

That's weird! Look at this table.

no. black frogs	no. moves
1	3
2	8
3	15
4	?

Is there a pattern here?

The 3 and the 15 are one less than a power of 2 ($3 = 2^2 - 1$, $15 = 2^4 - 1$) but the 8 ruins the pattern. Does that mean that there's one rule for the odd and one for the even? Or does it mean that we've got the 8 wrong? Or maybe, 4 frogs will take an even number of steps, say 24 or 32?

Where did 24 and 32 come from?

Step 5. We've **got** to do 4 frogs **now**. How did we get 15 moves for three frogs? We've just tried it again and we had to use 21 moves! Mind you some of the frogs had to back up and we don't remember doing that before.

At this stage there was silence, a lot of thinking and much experimentation for 20 minutes or so.

There must be a trick here somewhere. We're going to be in real trouble if we get two black frogs next to each other before the end of the game. So we've got to try to keep black and white next to each other in the middle of the board. With that strategy in mind, here goes nothing on four black frogs.

Find the key to the problem. We had this idea earlier didn't we?

W	W	W	W		B	B	B	B
W	W	W	W	B		B	B	B
W	W	W		B	W	B	B	B
W	W		W	B	W	B	B	B
W	W	B	W		W	B	B	B
W	W	B	W	B	W		B	B
W	W	B	W	B	W	B		B
W	W	B		B	W	B	W	B
W		B	W	B	W	B	W	B
	W	B	W	B	W	B	W	B
B	W		W	B	W	B	W	B
B	W	B	W		W	B	W	B
B	W	B	W	B	W		W	B
B	W	B	W	B	W	B	W	
B	W	B	W	B	W	B		W
B	W	B	W	B		B	W	W
B	W	B		B	W	B	W	W
B		B	W	B	W	B	W	W
B	B		W	B	W	B	W	W
B	B	B	W		W	B	W	W
B	B	B	W	B	W		W	W
B	B	B	W	B		W	W	W
B	B	B		B	W	W	W	W
B	B	B	B		W	W	W	W

Jump you blacks!

Alternate black and white

Jump you whites!

Remember to alternate!

Jump ye blacks!

Make a hole for the whites to jump

Now move the blacks along.

Slide white

Jump white.
Whites are home!
So are blacks.

It looks like it's 24 after all. So much for the powers of 2!

Step 6. Reflection. But that's opened up more questions than it's answered. Sure we've solved the original problem. We can certainly change the frogs over. But how do we know if we've done it in the fewest moves? How many moves will it take in the five frog case? Or in the five hundred frog case?

Our guess, of course is that with n frogs a side we'll manage to do it in n(n + 2) moves. But how to prove that we can do it in that many, and how to prove we can't do better than that many? **Better** still, how to prove **nobody** can do better than that many?

There are still problems to be solved here. That's infuriating! We don't like to give up on a problem! We hate it when that happens.

It would be nice to get the general picture. After all, this is what a mathematician would try to do.

What, in our experience, has prepared us for this? Will we have to give up on this one after getting quite a nice conjecture? Have we got far enough anyway?

Further Explorations

29. (a) What heuristics did you see being used in that case study? Were there any new ones?

   (b) What additional heuristics would you have used if you had been doing the problem? (You may want to go through the problem again and think about this as you go).

   (c) Bring your heuristics' file up to date.

30. (a) What evidence of metacognition did you see?

   (b) What metacognition was occurring in your own mind as you read through the problem?

   (c) What help would you have given the person in the case study to speed up the solution process?

31. Was any extra information used that wasn't contained in the original problem?

32. Rephrase the problem in your own words.

33. (a) How could you use an exhaustive search for this problem? Would you recommend this approach here?

    (b) Could you act out this problem?

    (c) What about guess and check. Could that be used?

    Note that one of the difficulties with modelling is that you forget to write down the moves you make.

34. The case study just mentioned in passing, a pattern of n(n + 2). Could the pattern be (n + 1)2 - 1? Can you justify either of those formulae?

35. How many moves would you need if there were 6 frogs on each side?

36. Can you think up any extensions or generalizations for this problem?

37. When is a problem finished? Would you have been happy with 24 as the answer for the four frog problem?

38. What was all the fuss about at the end of the case study? The problem had been solved hadn't it?

39. How would you use this problem in a primary school classroom? Would you use plastic frogs or counters? What do you think these students would gain from such a problem?

CHAPTER SUMMARY

In this chapter we used the following strategies:

13 puzzle

    use a diagram;
eliminate some possibilities;
be systematic;
list all possibilities;
trial and error;
use symmetry;
use algebra;
have I seen a problem like this before (Temple of Gloom).

handshakes

    try simpler problem;
use a table;
draw a diagram;
look for a pattern.

frogs

    use concrete materials;
use a diagram;
use a table;
look for a pattern;
use smaller cases;
act it out (might be fun);
by systematic.

The case studies we have used in this chapter are to give an idea of the thought processes that you may experience as you are solving problems. The real point here is that solutions to worthwhile problems do not appear without a great deal of effort.

CHAPTER 10 PATTERNS

1. THE STAMP PROBLEM

Sandra has a large collection of 5p and 7p stamps. She notices that she cannot make up a total of 8p by combining these stamps. She also notices that she can make 42p by using six 7p stamps or by using seven 5p stamps and a 7p stamp. She decides to find which amounts of postage can be made using only 5p and 7p stamps, and which amounts cannot.

Solve Sandra's problem.

Solution. Here is a good place to experiment. We'll draw up a table and place a tick for every amount that we can make. Amounts that we can't make will get a cross.

Amount	1	2	3	4	5	6	7	8	9	10	11	12	13	14	15	16
Doable	✗	✗	✗	✗	✔	✗	✔	✗	✗	✔	✗	✔	✗	✔	✔	✗

Amount	17	18	19	20	21	22	23	24	25	26	27	28	29	30	31	32
Doable	✔	✗	✔	✔	✔	✔	✗	✔	✔	✔	✔	✔	✔	✔	✔	✔

It's probably a good idea to tick off the easy amounts first. Obviously Sandra can make all multiples of 5 and 7 as well as multiples of 12. So the first obvious amounts follow the pattern 5, 10, 15, 20, 25,... and 7, 14, 21, 28, ... The other values take a bit of working out sometimes, especially if they can't be done.

Take 23, for instance. That needs a little bit of trial and error. It's clearly not a multiple of 5 or 7. So both 5 and 7 have to be used.

Suppose we use one 7. Then we have to get 16. But 16 isn't a multiple of 5, so we're going to have to use two 7s. Now 14 from 23 is 9 and it's clear that it can't be made with 5s and 7s. So 23 can't be made either. (And neither can 16.)

Doesn't that mean we can't get 30? If we use the same reasoning as before ... Ah! Since 30 is a multiple of 5, we can't say that we have to use 7. So the argument is different for 30.

Now in our table, there's a nice long string of ticks from 24 to 32. Does the string end somewhere? Where? Why? Perhaps we should try a few more values.

$33 = 5 + 4 \times 7;$ $34 = 4 \times 5 + 2 \times 7;$ $35 = 7 \times 5;$ $36 = 3 \times 5 + 3 \times 7;$
$37 = 6 \times 5 + 7;$ $38 = 2 \times 5 + 4 \times 7;$ $39 = 5 \times 5 + 2 \times 7;$ $40 = 8 \times 5 ...$

The string looks as if it is going on for ever. A pattern of never-ending totals. So let's

Conjecture: Sandra can make every amount from 24 upwards.

How can we possible prove that conjecture? Do we have to write down a way of getting every single amount? That's clearly impossible. But is there any other method?

Further Explorations

1. Can Sandra make up all amounts from 43 to 50?

2. Do you want to revise the Conjecture?

3. Is there some link between the numbers? How did you make up 43? Is that linked in any way to earlier numbers?

Perhaps you might have noticed that $39 = 32 + 7$. So if you can get 32 you can surely get 39. But $39 = 34 + 5$ and that might make our lives a little easier. This is because $40 = 35 + 5$, $41 = 36 + 5$, $42 = 37 + 5$ and $43 = 38 + 5$. How does that help? Can't we just keep adding 5s and go round the cycle again and again?

$44 = 39 + 5;$ $45 = 40 + 5:$ $46 = 41 + 5;$ $47 = 42 + 5;$ $48 = 43 + 5.$

This pattern looks as if it might go on for ever.

Further Explorations

4. Prove the Conjecture.

5. Actually solving the Conjecture is only the beginning of a potentially long haul here. We could start again with 5p and 9p stamps. What is the Conjecture in this case and how would you prove it?

6. With 5p and dp stamps would you conjecture that Sandra could get every amount from $4(d - 1)$ onwards? If you would how would you prove it? If you wouldn't what would you conjecture?

7. Suppose Sandra had mp and np stamps. What would you conjecture then?

8. In Exploration 6 did you make allowances for d possibly being a multiple of 5?

9. We have so far neglected the totals that you can't get with 5p and 7p stamps. Go back and have a look at them. There's a nice pattern involving the non-totals and 23. Check it out.

10. Can you solve this problem using a table like this one below?

	0	1	2	3	4	...
0	0	5	10	15	20	25
1	7	12	17	22	27	32
2	14	19	24	29	34	39
⋮						

Look for patterns in this table.

11. Reword Sandra's stamp problem.

12. Reword it again using the names of some children that you know and putting the question in a setting that you know they would enjoy.

13. How would you use Sandra's problem in class? (At what level and for what children? Would you give it to them to do individually or in groups, as homework or in class? How far would you go with it? Why?)

In this problem we started to see the original pattern by using a table. Lots of hard work may have enabled you to see the pattern (m − 1)(n − 1) and up for the mp and np case. A proof of that is really quite difficult.

2. SUPERMARKET CANS

Anaris is stacking cans in a supermarket (see below). He starts off by stacking 3 cans. His next stack needs 6 cans and the next 10. How many cans will he need for his 20th stack?

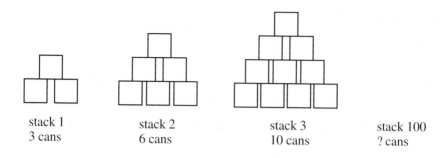

stack 1   stack 2   stack 3   stack 100
3 cans   6 cans   10 cans   ? cans

Solution. In Sandra's problem we thought there was a combination of 5 and 7 for every number bigger than or equal to 24. At first that seemed impossible. Here we only have to put together the 100th stack. We must be able to do that in a finite number of steps. But 100 seems so large that it's not likely to be easy. Anyway we may make some mistakes along the way if we tackle it head on. So let's tackle it nice and easily.

Let's do some experimenting then. And we'll complete a table as we go (Table 1).

stack number	number of cans
1	3
2	6
3	10
4	15
5	21
6	28
7	36
8	45

Table 1

Having laboriously worked things out to the 8th stack, can we get the 9th stack by cunning and guile? Is there a pattern here? If there is, can we justify it?

It's often useful to look at the difference between numbers in a table to see if you can find a pattern. The differences between successive numbers in the cans' column of the table are 3, 4, 5, 6, 7, 8, 9. Not such a hard pattern huh? The guess would be, that the 9th stack is equal to the 8th stack plus 10. So we'd expect 55 cans in the 9th stack. We'd also expect 55 + 11 = 66 cans in the 10th stack.

Further Explorations

14. Continue the table up to the 20th stack.

15. Your answer to the last question is probably correct if you haven't made any arithmetical errors. Check your answer and then convince a friend.

16. Can you find a slick way of adding up all the cans in the 20th stack?

17. Why should this pattern exist?

    Can you justify it?

18. In Table 1, notice that if you multiply an odd stack number by the number before it, you get a number in the can's column. What is the pattern here? Does it extend to even numbers?

The interesting thing about Anaris's second stack is that it's the first stack with 3 cans added on the bottom. A similar thing can be said for the third stack. If you take away the first row of cans you've got the second stack. The first row has 4 cans. So the third stack is the second stack plus 4. This pattern goes on and on. The eleventh stack is the tenth stack plus however many cans there are in the bottom row.

This gives us the following:

$$\text{stack } 1 = 1 + 2$$

$$\text{stack } 2 = \underbrace{1 + 2}_{\text{stack 1}} + \underbrace{3}_{\text{row 1}}$$

$$\text{stack } 3 = \underbrace{1 + 2 + 3}_{\text{stack 2}} + \underbrace{4}_{\text{row 1}}$$

$$\text{stack } 4 = 1 + 2 + 3 + 4 + 5$$

The pattern here shows that

stack 15 = 1 + 2 + 3 + 4 + 5 + 6 + 7 + 8 + 9 + 10 + 11 + 12 + 13 + 14 + 15 and stack 20 = 1 + 2 + 3 + ... + 21.

But at the moment we don't have a simple way of adding up the numbers from 1 to 21. Can that only be done directly? Where's your cunning.

Further Explorations

19. Copy and complete the following

    stack 20   = 1 +   2 +   3 +   + 19 + 20 + 21

    stack 20   = 21 + 20 + 19 +   + 3   +   2 +   1.

    If we add these up we get

    2 stack 20 = (1 + 21) + (2 + 20) +   + (20 + 2) + (21 + 1)

                 = 22 + 22 +   + 22 + 22

    How many 22s are there? So

    2 stack 20 = 22 ×   .

    But this gives

    stack 20   = 11 ×   .

    So stack 20   =   .   Just what you got in Exploration 14, hopefully.

20. Find the number of cans in the 100th stack.

21. Reword Anaris's can problem.

22. Reword again using the names of some children that you know and putting the question in a setting you know they would enjoy.

23. How would you use Anaris' problem in class?

24. What heuristics were used in solving Anaris' problem?

3. THE CHESSBOARD

How many squares are there on a chessboard?

Solution. That doesn't look too bad. A chessboard has 8 squares along each side. So it has $8 \times 8 = 64$ squares.

Hmmm. That seems too easy. Can we get away with that? Have we missed something? It's true that a chessboard has 64 squares. Is there something wrong with my interpretation of "square" then? Could the question mean something more than the obvious squares? What other squares can there be? Hmmm. Two black squares together with two white squares make a square. If you like, they make a 2×2 square. Have I got to count all those? **And** the 3×3 ones too?!

Suppose then we have to count all the $1 \times 1, 2 \times 2, 3 \times 3, 4 \times 4, 5 \times 5, 6 \times 6, 7 \times 7$ and 8×8 squares. Can we do that correctly the first time up? What other strategy could we use.

Before we think about that we're going to get some practice in on small "chessboards" . For instance, how many squares are there on a 2×2 board?

There are clearly four 1×1 squares and one 2×2 squares, so that gives us 5 squares in all.

So how about the $3 ¥ 3$ board? It's easy enough to see that there are nine 1×1 squares and a $3 ¥ 3$ square but the 2×2 squares might be a tad more difficult. We'll draw a diagram and count them from that.

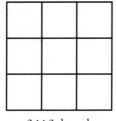

3×3 board.

Looks like four 2×2 squares. So there are $9 + 4 + 1 = 14$ squares on the 3×3 board.

We'll just do one more. The 4×4 board. Ah. Maybe it's time to draw up a table.

Further Explorations

25. How many squares are there on a 4×4 board?

    How many squares are there on a 5×5 board?

26. Draw up a table to display the evidence that we've got so far.

27. Are there any patterns emerging?

◆ ◆ ◆ ◆

In Anaris' problem, when we were counting the cans, we looked at the difference between totals and found that the differences went like 3, 4, 5, 6, 7, ... The differences increased by one at every step.

In this wretched squares problem, the differences are 4, 9, 16, 25, ... Something more complicated is happening here.

Further Explorations

28. What pattern is lurking in the numbers 4, 9, 16, 25? What is the next number in this sequence?

29. Use the pattern you discovered in the last Exploration to extend the table up to the 8 × 8 board.

30. Can you justify the pattern you've been using?

◆ ◆ ◆ ◆

While we're doing things directly, let's try to work out the number of squares on a 12 × 12 board. Try this for yourselves by working up from the 8 × 8 board. Then follow the argument below.

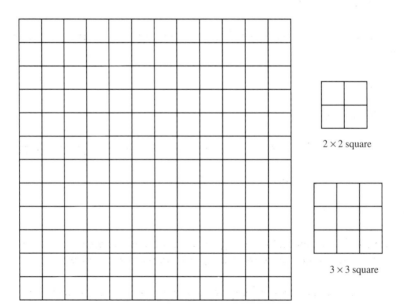

the 12 × 12 square

2 × 2 square

3 × 3 square

Step 1   How many 1×1 squares?

That's easy, $12 \times 12 = 144$.

Step 2   How many 2×2 squares?

How can we find all the 2×2 squares? We have to do this systematically. If you look at the 12×12 board, every place where two lines cross, is the centre of a 2×2 square. If we count all these crossing places we'll have the number of 2×2 squares.

Now we, of course, can count them one by one. Better still, notice that they form an 11×11 square. So there are $11 \times 11 = 121$ crossings. That means there are 121 2×2 squares.

Step 3   How many 3×3 squares?

Following on from Step 2, there is a square in the middle of a 3×3 square. So every square on the 12×12 board is the centre of a 3×3 square.

Hang on! That's patently absurd. But it's almost true. It's true for all the squares not on the outside of the 12×12 square. Now these "inside" squares form a 10×10 square. Obviously we have $10 \times 10 = 100$ 3×3 squares.

Step 4   How many 4×4 squares?

Something to do with the number of crossings on the 12×12 square but two rows or columns in?

Further Explorations

31. Finish off Step 4.

32. Step 5 aims to find all the 5×5 squares. Can you do that systematically?

33. Find the number of squares on a 12×12 board.

34. Reword the squares problem.

35. Reword the squares problem using the names of some children that you know and putting the question in a setting that you know they would enjoy.

36. Is there some neat way of adding up all these squares? Perhaps something like the method in Explorations 19 of the can problem?

◆ ◆ ◆ ◆

To try to get an idea of how to count the number of squares in any size chessboard, let's start by extending the table of Exploration 26. Let's study the numbers in this table (Table 2) to try to see if we can pick up any patterns.

size of board	number of squares
1	1
2	5
3	14
4	30
5	55
6	91
7	140

Table 2

We've already realised that the differences here are squares. This enables us to answer the original question (how many squares on a chess board), by adding 64 to 140. The answer is 204. But how do we find the number of squares in a 12×12 board?

Taking differences got us started. How about trying division now? Divide the entry in the number of squares column by the size of the board. Unfortunately in the second row 2 doesn't go into 5 exactly and then neither does 3 go into 14. But the division does give us some interesting fractions (see Table 3).

size of board	number of squares	quotient
1	1	1
2	5	5/2
3	14	14/3
4	30	15/2
5	55	11
6	91	91/6
7	140	20
8	204	51/2

Table 3

The only thing we can see there is that the denominator in the quotient is always 1, 2, 3 or 6. Well, it's 1, 2, 3 or 6 so far. Let's assume for the moment that it's always one of those. Put in a new column in the table which is 6 times the quotient and we might get rid of all those fractions.

Further Explorations

37. Add a column headed "6 × quotient" in the last table. Put all eight entries in this column. Can you see any pattern in the numbers in this column?

    Try the divising strategy again?

38. So 2 doesn't go into 15, but it does go into 6. And 3 doesn't go into 28 but it does go into 15. What pattern does this suggest?

39. Find the number of squares in a 12 × 12 board by working back from the last exercise through the "6 × quotient" to an answer.

    Does this agree with your answer to Exploration 33?

    If the numbers don't agree, which one is correct and why? Correct the incorrect value.

◆ ◆ ◆ ◆

So we've noticed that the 6 × quotient column is made up of two factors. One of these factors is the size of the next board in the table. The other is one more than twice the side of the board we're working on.

In algebraic terms, for the n × n board,

$$6 \times \text{quotient} = (n + 1)(2n + 1)$$

$$\backslash \quad \text{quotient} = \frac{(n + 1)(2n + 1)}{6}$$

$$\backslash \quad \frac{\text{number of squares}}{n} = \frac{(n + 1)(2n + 1)}{6}$$

$$\backslash \quad \text{numbers of squares} = \frac{n(n + 1)(2n + 1)}{6}$$

Further Explorations

40. How many squares on a 112 × 112 board?

41. Reword the problem for some children you know. Put it in a context they would enjoy.

42. Use the curriculum document to decide how you could use this problem for children at different levels. How far would you take the problem at each of these levels?

43. What heuristics and metacognition have you used during this problem?

44. Now you know how to answer the question, what scaffolding would have been helpful at what stages?

45. How many rectangles are there in a 10 × 12 board?

    Can you find the answer for any rectangular board?

4. MATCHES

Sarah is playing with matches. It's not to be recommended but she isn't striking any. She's just putting them down on the table to make triangles. She finds that she can make four triangles with 9 matches. How many matches will she need to make 100 triangles?

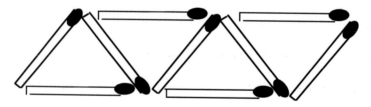

Solution. Let's try to make a table. We know that 4 triangles need 9 matches. So how many matches do we need to make 1, 2, 3 and so on triangles?

Further Explorations

46. By extending Sarah's matchstick diagram out to the right, complete the following table.

number of triangles	number of matches
1	
2	
3	
4	9
5	

47. What's the pattern in this table?

   How many matches are needed for 10 triangles?

   How many matches are needed for 100 triangles?

48. Give a simple rule which will tell you how many matches you need once you are given the number of triangles.

49. How many triangles can you make with 99 matches?

50. Why haven't we used an even number of matches yet?

51. But Sarah suddenly realises that she can make six triangles with fewer than 13 matches. What is the smallest number of matches she needs to make six triangles?

52. Can seven squares be made up with 14 matches?

   Can ten squares be made up with 20 matches?

   Can any number of squares be made up with twice that number of matches?

53. Can you do better than this even? What's the most triangles you can make with 18 matches?

   How about with 19 matches?

5. DOMINO HOUSES

Mahia has broken the world record for building domino houses. She built a domino house 73 storeys high. In the picture there is a 4 storey house which uses 24 dominoes. How many dominoes did Mahia need to break the world record?

Solution. Have you seen something like this before? Looks very cannish to me. But let's draw up a table first and see how much progress we can make that way.

Further Explorations

54. Make a table with one column for the number of storeys and one for the number of dominoes. Take the number of storeys up to 7. Complete the table.

55. How do you get from a building to one with one more storey?

56. How many dominoes are needed in a 10 storey house?

57. What's the pattern here? How can we quickly find the number of dominoes in a 100 storey house?

58. Answer Mahia's problem.

59. Invent a problem similar to this one (and/or the can problem of Anaris).

    Solve the problem as far as you are able.

60. If you were using this problem with 8 year old children, how would you introduce it? Would you expect them to use equipment to solve it, or make a drawing or use guess and check? Could they do it some other way?

6. SIGNALS

The computer works by sending messages that could be thought of as finite strings of zeros and ones. A new XantnaX supercomputer uses strings of zeros and ones but, for technical reasons, never sends a message containing two consecutive zeros. How many different messages can it send which are 40 characters long? Each character is, of course, a zero or a one.

Solution. In this chapter you must be getting used to making up tables so let's do the same thing here (see Table 4).

number of characters	possible messages	number of messages
1	0	2
	1	
2	01	3
	10	
	11	
3	010	5
	011	
	101	
	110	
	101	

Table 4

Further Explorations

61. Continue the table to include messages with 7 characters.

62. Is there any pattern in your table?

    (Analyse the number of messages using the techniques that have been introduced in this chapter.)

63. Use your answer to the last Exploration to calculate the number of messages with 8 characters. Is this the number you get by direct enumeration of all those messages? If not find out which method is incorrect and why and correct it.

64. Can you justify the patterns you produced in Exploration 60? Or, if you had to correct it in Exploration 61, can you justify your latest patterns?

65. Have you seen the numbers in the third column of your table before? What have they got to do with rabbits, 1202 and the Italian city of Pisa?

66. These numbers are also related to sunflower seeds and pineapples. Look up Fibonacci numbers and find out the connection.

67. Some other mathematicians you may have heard of are Euclid, Newton, Kovalevskaya, Noether and Aitken. Look them up in an encyclopaedia. Which one has a New Zealand connection?

7. CHAPTER SUMMARY

In this chapter we have used the following strategies:

Stamps
>   make a table;
>   be systematic;
>   generalize or extend.

Supermarket cans
>   try a simpler problem;
>   use a table;
>   look for patterns;
>   generalize.

Chessboard
>   try a simpler problem
>   look for patterns
>   generalize.

Matches
>   use a table;
>   look for patterns;
>   generalize.

Domino houses
>   try simpler cases;
>   use a table;
>   look for patterns;
>   generalize.

Signals
>   use a table;
>   try simpler cases;
>   look for patterns;
>   generalize.

The aim of this chapter was to look at a range of similar problems which involve finding patterns. We looked at various approaches and at ways of being certain that the patterns we found were correct.

CHAPTER 11 AN OVERVIEW

1. INTRODUCTION

So far we have spent a lot of time and several chapters playing around with a number of problems. Along the way we've picked up a few ideas regarding problem solving. We've talked about heuristics, metacognition and scaffolding. In this chapter we look at solving problems in general, from a holistic point of view. Here we try to set out the key steps of problem solving as they apply to any problem.

Once again we need to make the point that, although we set these steps out one after the other, it is in fact very rare for them to follow this way in practice. In most problems you will need to dodge backwards and forwards among the key steps before the penny drops and you get both an answer and a solution.

2. GETTING STARTED

This is the first part of problem solving and covers Pólya's first two phases.

(1) Understand the problem. The problem will either be presented in writing or verbally. If it is in writing the solver has to *read the problem* and read it carefully. Many a solver has begun by solving a problem they thought was there rather than the one that was actually there. Often this turns out to be a problem they did recently.

As the solvers read the problem they should be asking the various questions posed by Pólya. They should also be *looking for key words*. These are words which, if changed, will lead to a quite different problem. They are words or phrases which are essential in the solution of the problem.

Some teachers we know of use a highlighter to draw attention to these key words when they are working in front of their class. This encourages the children to do the same as they start to work on a problem. Highlighting, underlining or some other device helps the children to focus on the problem as well as to focus their thinking.

Consider this problem. Peter is 18 years older than his daughter Sue who is 7 years old. How old will Peter be when he is twice as old as Sue?

In this problem, "18", "7" and "twice as old" are all key words or phrases. The question, and more importantly the answer, is altered if any one of these is changed. On the other hand, "Peter" could be "Peta" and "Sue", "Sam" without changing the answer or the method of solution.

One of the metacognitive aspects of problem solving is to know when to come back to the original problem and read it again. This may be necessary to see if you are on the track of a solution or if you have inadvertently started to solve another problem. It may also help you to try another approach if you have made no progress with a particular method of attack.

Another useful strategy at this point is to reword the problem. This helps the problem solver to think about the key points of the problem. A comparison between the actual problem and the reworded problem may well reveal a discrepancy that could have wasted the solver's time.

(2) Think. Apart from the metacognition already discussed in Section 4, which largely related to control, at the start of a problem it is necessary for solvers to go through a mental list of heuristics in an effort to find a few which will get them started.

It is also worth asking the following Pólya questions (Pólya, 1973, p. xvif).

> What is the unknown?
> What are the data?
> Is drawing a figure useful?

> Is there a related problem that has been solved before?
> Could it be used here?

> In addition it is worth considering:

> What area of mathematics can be used?
> (algebra, geometry, number, etc)
> What approaches might work?

In the Peter and Sue problem, the unknown is Peter's age when he is twice as old as Sue. The data are the current age of the pair. We don't think a diagram is helpful ourselves, but we have seen this problem done using a number line. Is this problem like anything we've seen before?

The problem looks more like a number or an algebra problem than a geometric one. We'll leave you to think what approaches might work.

(3) Experiment. This is often an early stage in the problem solving process. It has two main functions. The first is to get a feel for the problem. The second is to start to produce some evidence for a conjecture. The experiments may be calculations or measurements or a variety of things depending on the problem in hand. We've experimented many times in the earlier chapters of this book.

The experiments should be **systematic**. Metacognition should be used at each stage to guide the experiments. The aim is to get central, useful information that can be collated in some way, rather than an unconnected jumble of, say, numbers. We say more about this under guess and check in Section 4.

The results of experiments should be **recorded** in some logical fashion. Perhaps consider the case n = 1, then n = 2 and so on. Numbers should not be arbitrarily scattered at random over the page. The data should be kept in a **list**, **table** or **diagram**. It is worth keeping these experiments until the problem has been completely solved. They may well be useful to provide or inspire a counterexample later. It is almost certain that the moment after you have thrown some data away, you will need it.

(4) Symmetry. This is something that can be exploited at **all** stages of the problem solving process. When it exists it means that an awful lot of repetitive work can be done away with.

There are a couple of places that we've used symmetry. Remember the equilateral triangle of the Temple of Gloom. By symmetry we can choose any corner vertex to start with. Similarly, we cut down the possibilities in the 13-puzzle by realising that there was an axis of symmetry through the centre of the diagram with the 9 squares.

(5) Panic. This is a common feeling at the start of a new problem. Success and experience will give the solver confidence to continue. However, even expert problem solvers face panic on occasions. It's a perfectly natural reaction. One of the aims of practising problem solving is to gain the confidence to know that you can solve problems. So when the panic attack comes, say "I can solve it" and move on.

Further Explorations

1. Reread the first part of Chapter 6. How were the features of the section about "Getting Started", applied to the Temple of Gloom problem?

2. Where in the main problem of Chapter 7 did we need to "think" at the getting started stage?

3. Name three problems where "experiment" was a useful initial strategy.

4. Have we ever used symmetry in any of the problems so far?

5. Name two occasions when you panicked when you first read a problem.

6. In which problems did we need to make a list, draw up a table or use a diagram?

3. CONJECTURING

(1) Pattern. This can be the most enjoyable and interesting part of the problem solving process. In more difficult problems, it is necessary to find a **pattern, rule** or some **sort of relation** in order to produce a conjecture. We spent the whole of the last chapter looking for patterns.

As we have already said, some problems give up the correct conjecture immediately (that for the Four Colour Theorem was discovered by a teenager in one evening). Other problems take more time. In harder problems it may be necessary to discard a number of conjectures before obtaining the right one. Some people find some problems easier to make conjectures about than others. Conjectures require practice. So it is necessary to start with simple problems and work up.

(2) Sense. Does the conjecture make sense? Is it **consistent** with previous knowledge and the data that has been assembled in the experimental phase. Does the conjecture imply anything that **feels wrong**? Intuition and common sense can and should be used here. A conjecture which implies that a boy weighs 1000 kgms must surely be wrong. Any conjecture should be **justifiable**. Even though it cannot be proved at this stage, there should be good reasons for choosing one conjecture over another.

Further Explorations

7. What was the pattern in the frog problem (Chapter 9)? How was the pattern discovered?

8. (a) Give an example of a problem in which a pattern was discovered through the use of a table.

    (b) Give an example of a problem in which the pattern was discovered by a method other than using a table.

    (c) Could the pattern discovered in the problem in (a) have been discovered without using a table? How could it have been discovered?

    (d) Could the pattern discovered in the problem in (b) have been discovered by using a table? Justify your assertion.

9. (a) What nonsensical conjectures have we made in this book?

    (b) What nonsensical conjectures have you made to problems in this book?

4. PROOF/COUNTEREXAMPLE

Right at the outset we'd better say that when we say proof we don't really mean proof, we mean justification. Think of the proof line (see Figure 1). At the far right end there is absolute and irrefutable proof. That's what mathematicians seek all the time.

Moving to the left from proof there are weaker forms of proof which are better called justifications. And justifications cover a wide range.

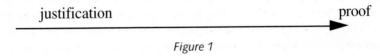

Figure 1

Euclid had a good, watertight proof that the angles in a triangle add up to 180°. We won't go into it here. Please believe us that he did. But if you cut out a triangle, tear off two corners and join them to the third corner, the angles "look" as if they make a straight line. A straight line has 180°. So the angle sum of a triangle is 180°. (See Figure 2.)

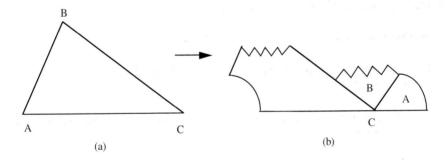

Figure 2

That's a nice justification. It's suitable for children of a certain age but it's not exactly a proof. First, it is a demonstration on a particular triangle. Second, if we put the protractor on Figure 2 (b) at C, we couldn't be sure that the angle was exactly 180°.

We do believe, however, that justifications start young. Even children new to school can justify things to satisfy themselves. They start at the left hand side of our proof line in Figure 1. As they progress, the sophistication of their justifications should increase. Eventually some of them will get well down to the right hand end of the line.

Now it may be that even the topmost mathematicians haven't got proof really sorted out yet. Possibly, if we could come back in a 1000 years, we would have a much deeper concept to deal with. (That's a scary thought.) So we are happy to think of proof as the justifications that we, you or your children can handle at this time. However, we hope that we can push ourselves (as well as you and your children) further and further to the right of the proof line.

The more difficult problems will require the solver to trade off conjecture against proofs against counterexamples. The process is a dynamic one which is only completed when the final step in the solution is written down. Frequently trying to prove a conjecture gives an idea for a counterexample and looking for a counterexample can give an idea for a proof. Whether starting in the proof or counterexample direction the solver may see that the conjecture needs adjusting and the process starts again.

It is difficult to see whether to first try to justify a conjecture or show it is wrong. The decision as to which to try first depends on the solver and the problem. If testing a few cases will cover all possible counterexamples then the solver should go that route. This will either produce a counterexample or strongly confirm the conjecture. In the latter case, of course, a proof will still be required.

Some problems look like others and this may suggest a way to proceed to a proof. A slight change of a known proof might work. Or the problem may be one which suggests a well known proof technique such as **proof by contradiction** or **mathematical induction**.

(1) Extreme Cases. In trying to find a counterexample it is often valuable to try **extreme examples** or **extreme cases**. These examples are somehow at the edge of the spectrum of values that are being used. For instance, what happens if a number is very small or what happens as n approaches infinity? What happens if the triangle is isosceles? Extreme cases are usually easier to handle than more general situations so it is worth testing a few before trying a proof. Even if they do not provide a counterexample, they may well give the solver some useful information which can be used later.

If we were seeking a generalisation for the Temple of Gloom problem, we might ask if the numbers 1, 2, 3, 4, 5, 100 could be used. The 100 here surely makes this an extreme case.

(2) Special Cases. A conjecture can also be tested against **special cases** rather than extreme cases. Special cases are typical, particular cases such as the ones used during the experimental phase. Where possible, cases should be tested because they are straight forward or easy to test. But sometimes more complicated cases are forced on the solver.

(3) Simpler problem. Sometimes problems are far too difficult to solve first time. They may involve far too many variables to be able to comprehend. In that case reduce the problem to a **simpler problem** in some way. For instance, a gambling problem involving five dice might be reduced at first to one involving only two. Insight gained from the two

dice case may well lead to the solution of the original problem. Here the aim is to keep as many of the essentials of the problem as possible while reducing the problem to a manageable size.

It was too hard for us to find all the squares on a chessboard straight away. So we looked at smaller boards first. These were simpler in the context of the problem. Remember with the frog problem of Chapter 9, we first tried one frog a side and then two.

(4) Exhaust All Possibilities. One of the very simplest methods of proof is to **exhaust all possibilities**. If there are sufficiently few cases to handle (under fifty, say), then by looking at each one in turn, the solver can learn about the entire problem. This way any conjecture about the situation is immediately verified or disproven. Simple combinatorial problems such as the behaviour of two dice are often open to this approach. It could be used on the Temple of Gloom problem too.

When a solution has been obtained by older children by the exhaustive approach, it is worth asking the Pólya phase four question "Can you derive the result differently?" They should be looking for more sophisticated approaches. There are times, however, when no other method is available.

(5) Guess And Check. One of the simplest ways of tackling a problem is via **guess and check**. This is sometimes also called **trial and error**. In the problem of Peter and Sue, an answer can be found by guessing and checking. It is therefore a good strategy for simple problems. There are drawbacks, however. First, if the problem involved has a large number of cases, for instance the five dice gambling game we alluded to earlier, then it may not be easy to guess the correct answer in a reasonable time. Second, although guessing and checking will give an answer, the method cannot tell you whether the answer is unique. It may well be that the problem has a number of answers. Only an exhaustive search will be able to determine all answers in such a problem. Finally, the guess and check method in complicated situations may only reveal the conjecture required. It may not justify that conjecture. The efficiency of guess and check can be increased with metacognition by using **guess and improve**. Here subsequent guesses are improved using the data of past guesses. Again in simple problems where a unique answer is almost certain, this is a useful strategy. For instance, young primary school children (6 and 7 years old) were asked how many mini vans were required to transport 88 children if 7 children travelled in each van. Many children guessed and checked until they hit on 13. However, at that age they did not seem to be able to use previous guesses to obtain a closer guess the next time. Their guesses were quite random. So this may be an heuristic which works better with older children.

It is perhaps worth noting here that in some ways the whole of problem solving is guess and check. A conjecture is a guess and the proof of the conjecture could be interpreted as a check. The level of cognition in this generality, of course, may be very high. Normally guess and check is thought of at a reasonably unsophisticated level.

(6) Definitions. Quite often it is useful to **define** something in the middle of solving a problem. A definition reduces the number of words that need to be used and greatly aids the speed of communication.

(7) Notation. In the same way a good **notation** can be invaluable. Great strides were made in arithmetic with the introduction of a symbol for zero. Changing from words to algebra was also a great stride forward. Notation can help in many problem solving exercises. We saw this with Snakeye Sam's problem and the frog problem.

Diagrams work in a similar way to convey information efficiently at almost every point in the problem solving process. Again we used diagrams with Snakeye's dice, the handshake problem and several others.

(8) Work Backwards. A technique that is sometimes useful is to **work backward** from the answer. This method is a way of gaining inspiration for a proof. It is also worth considering in other types of problems, particularly two-person games. The game of Nim, for instance, is well worth analysing this way in order to find a winning strategy. Once you have a conjecture it's often useful to see what that implies and what that is implied by. This may move you to another conjecture that is easier to prove.

(9) All Information. If you are unable to make any headway it is often worth rereading the question in an attempt to ensure that all of the information given in the problem has been used. Sometimes there is an implicit detail that is not mentioned specifically but which is vital to the solution. Knowing general facts not stated in the problem, such as the sum of the dots on opposite sides of a dice is 7, may well be required to solve a problem.

(10) Check. Having obtained a complete solution you should go through the justification and check every step. Even if the proof passes the check test, sometimes you still have a nagging doubt. In all cases it is a good idea for you to get someone else to check your solutions. At this stage too, sometimes you may see a quicker more efficient way to solve the problem. The new method needs to be written down and checked too.

Further Explorations

10. Give examples of problems where you found that looking for a proof of a conjecture showed a counterexample and where looking for a counterexample showed the way to a proof.

11. What problems used extreme cases to look for counterexamples?

12. When did we test a conjecture against a special case?

13. When did we find a simpler problem a useful strategy to try?

14. Give an example of a problem where exhausting all possibilities gave a proof.

15. Show how to use guess and improve in two problems stated earlier in this book.

16. Where did we use definitions to avoid using a lot of words?

17. Have we ever used notation to good effect?

18. In which problems did we find it useful to work backwards?

19. Did we ever need to go back to the original problem to discover a piece of information that we had overlooked?

20. Which problems relied on the fact that we had information from everyday life at our fingertips which was not expressly written into the problem?

21. Have we ever found an improved method to use on a problem that we've already solved?

5. GENERALIZATION/EXTENSION

(1) Generalization. A **generalization** is a problem which contains the original problem as a special case. Generalizations can often be found by increasing the number of digits (in some number problems), stepping up the dimension (in a geometry problem) or by increasing the number of variables in some way.

The reason for considering generalizations is that they give a result which is true for a much wider class of objects. One difficulty with generalizations is that they may require a quite different justification from the justification used in the original problem.

(2) Extension. An **extension** of a problem is one which is related to the original problem but not by way of a generalization. It may be that a problem can be extended by changing addition to multiplication. Extensions can be found by changing one of the conditions of the original problem in some way. As with generalizations, the proof of an extension may not be linked in any way to the proof of the original problem.

Further Explorations

22. Generalize five of the problems in this book.

23. Find extensions for five of the problems in this book.

6. GIVE UP

(1) Why? Some problems are too difficult to be solved right now. So, at times, you and your pupils will have to abandon some problems. If you are forced to abandon **all** problems you tackle, then the problems are too difficult.

(2) When? This will depend on the teacher and the children. It becomes a matter of priorities. However, any reasonable problem will take more than 10 minutes and less than 2 hours (unless it is an extended investigation). In general, we suspect that children can go further than we usually expect. This is especially true of the more able ones.

Actually we are still working on the frog problem and hope to have it licked ready for the next edition of this book.

(3) Help. In cases where the problem is too hard for both the teacher and the class, outside help should be summoned. This may be from another teacher, a book or a local university. We have to admit that we've posted the frog problem on a board at the local university. No luck yet though!

Further Explorations

24. Give two examples where problems in this book caused us or you to give up.

25. Give two examples of problems that many mathematicians had to give up on over the years.

7. SOME MODELS FOR TEACHING

In the previous sections we have outlined the theory of problem solving. Here and in the next section we consider the implementation of the teaching of problem solving. We are very definitely of the opinion that there are many ways to teach problem solving and teachers will undoubtedly develop the approach which is most comfortable for them and most appropriate for the particular children in a particular class.

There appear to be two extremes of problem solving teaching styles. On the one hand, some teachers will prefer to teach specific strategies and follow this up by giving children practice in using these strategies with some particular problems. At the other extreme, teachers may give children problems to tackle with no guidance on solution methods. Indeed, teachers may not even make their class aware of the names of the strategies that they have used in solving the problems.

There seems to be general belief though that children should be given the names of processes that they were using. If a process is named, then it enables children to recall it more quickly. It also enables more efficient communication between teacher and child and between child and child. By naming processes, children are more aware of the processes they use and are more likely to recall having used the process on a previous occasion. This is important given the usefulness of asking the question "have I seen a problem like this before?"

The amount of guidance that children need to be given will vary depending on their experience and ability. Perhaps senior classes and children who are mathematically more able, require less guidance. Junior classes and weaker pupils will undoubtedly need more help if they are to become successful problem solvers. It is important that children realise that there are general strategies that can be used in problem solving and that each individual problem does not need to be tackled by a new and different technique. "Friday afternoon puzzles" have the danger that children will not realise the importance and relevance of problem solving both inside and outside of mathematics.

Teaching specific strategies followed by practice may lead to teachers keeping a tight rein on the problem solving process. This may stultify children and block opportunities to explore and be creative. However, it may be necessary with very young children or with less able children of any age. Teachers could perhaps begin with this more closed style but become more open as they and their class gain confidence.

Each extreme we have mentioned then, has its advantages and disadvantages and should be used when appropriate.

The outline of a problem solving lesson which seems to be successful is given below.

- pose problem in whole class setting
- children work in groups of two or three
- teacher moves round the class
- whole class instruction given as needed
- report back session at the end

Especially in the early part of the year, or when a new heuristic is being introduced, it is worthwhile posing the question to the whole class. Before the children begin work on the problem, they will gain from some general discussion. It is important that they internalise the problem. The problem has to be made their problem. They have to "own" it, understand it and feel confident with it. This will come only with practice. Eventually children should be able to do this largely independently of the teachers.

We suggest that children begin work on problems in small groups of at most three per group. This means that a given class may have a large number of groups that may not all be serviced in one lesson. Bigger groups tend to be less efficient for children. Either the groups go off-task or they break up into smaller groups. Depending on the task, even groups of size four can effectively break up into two groups of two.

The crucial part of the teacher's interaction with children during the group phase, is the scaffolding provided. We discuss this in greater depth in the next chapter.

At least in the first instance, we would recommend that all children be given the same problem. This makes it easier for both the teacher and the class. The teacher will be faced with less variation this way. Undoubtedly some groups will have the same difficulties and these will then be easier to identify and react to. As a result the children will be better served by the teacher. If all of the class is attempting the same problem, the reporting back session at the end of the lesson has more point. There is no value in listening to your peers reporting back on a problem which you have not had to tackle.

Both during and at the end of the lesson, the teacher can take the ideas that the children have produced and help them to tidy them up and summarise them. The teacher should draw out all the strategies the class has used and note them for future use. It should be recognised that many problems can be solved in more than one way and that each has different merits. Children should be given other problems on which to practice any new strategies so that they are not forgotten.

With fixed periods for different subjects, secondary school classes will not always neatly finish at the end of a problem. It is worth having a closing session before the bell to report progress to date, which children still remember what they have been working on.

8. WHEN IS A PROBLEM SOLVED?

It's totally unclear how to answer this question. There seems to be at least five answers, (i) when you have got an answer to the problem; (ii) when you have a solution to the problem; (iii) when you have a nice solution to the problem; (iv) when you have generalized or extended the problem; (v) never. Let's look as these in turn.

When you have an answer. Traditionally in school this is where we have stopped. The end point is the result of many years of teaching algorithms. When you've been taught an algorithm (addition, long division, differentiation, whatever), you usually practice it on several examples. If you get the "right" answer often enough, then it is assumed that you've mastered the algorithm.

Problem solving isn't like learning algorithms, however. Getting an answer is only the first step. In many cases, "getting an answer" is really only finding a conjecture. You may remember in the frog problem that we got upset because we couldn't justify the pattern that we saw. Just because we could move teams of 2 frogs in 2 ¥ 4 moves and 3 frogs in 3 ¥ 5 moves and 4 frogs in 4 ¥ 7 moves, we could not be sure that this was always the case. Perhaps there was a better way. Perhaps teams of 2 frogs could be moved in fewer than 8 moves.

When you have a solution. A solution is better than an answer because a solution shows that you can justify the answer. This is a crucial step that many teachers omit in both their regular teaching and their problem solving teaching. Until you have justified your answer, you really haven't finished. Actually you've only just started.

If you are just content with an answer you may miss answers. Take the Temple of Gloom problem for example. It's not difficult to guess some answers. Without a solution though, you can't be sure that you've got all possible answers.

The solution of the farmyard leg problem which requires the animals to put their spare legs in the air, immediately gives you an answer and justifies it. It also gives you some insight into why that particular answer is correct.

So you can justifiably take a pause when you have a solution.

When you have a nice solution. We may be in "give up" territory here. "Nice" solutions don't always exist or if they do, they may not be found in our life time. There are many famous examples of deep mathematical results which fall in this category. Remember the Four Colour Theorem.

But we are in good company (Pólya's fourth phase includes this), when we suggest that it's at least worth thinking about nicer solutions that the one you have just found. You may find that a "better" solution gives you more insight into the problem. It may tell you more about what's going on. (Check out the various approaches to the animal legs and the 13-puzzle.) It may give you another useful weapon to use in a problem down the track.

If you can find a nice solution though, you can justifiably take a pause.

When you have a generalization or extension. Now it would be great to do this if you can. But we may need to "give up" right here. Although it is sometimes easy to invent generalizations or extensions, it is usually much harder to solve them than it is to solve the original problem.

Again Pólya, and others, would urge you on. It's certainly the mathematical thing to do. A true mathematician is always looking out for a generalization or extension to push the frontiers of the subject back just that bit further. So this is an honourable and admirable goal.

If you can find a generalization or extension and then prove it, then you can justifiably take a pause.

Never. Who said a mathematician's work is never done?   It's just one generalization/extension after another. Although we all of us have to give up sometimes (mortality seems to have an influence on this), the collective body of mathematicians never sleeps. It's always pushing ever onward.

So there is a sense in which a good problem is never completely solved. People just keep working at it and using it as a stepping stone to the next problem and the next and the ...

Further Exploration

26. Discuss the five stopping points above with respect to three of the problems in this book.

So mathematics goes on. And as far as we can tell at the moment, it will go on for ever and then some. Maybe no problem is ever truly solved. Ain't that a depressing thought!

9. CHAPTER SUMMARY

In this chapter we have gone through the major stages of problem solving and investigations, and listed some key points. These are

Getting started
> understand the problem;
> think;
> experiment;
> use symmetry;
> panic!

Conjecturing
> look for patterns;
> use common sense.

Proof/Counterexample

>try extreme cases;
>try special cases;
>try simpler problems;
>exhaust all possibilities;
>guess and check;
>use definitions;
>use notation;
>work backwards;
>use all the information;
>check your answer.

Generalization/Extension

>definition of generalization;
>definition of extension.

Give Up

>why;
>when;
>seek help.

We also suggest the following outlines of a problem solving lesson.

>pose problem in whole class setting;
>children work in groups of two or three;
>teacher moves round the class;
>whole class instruction/discussion given as needed;
>report back session at the end.

Finally we discussed when a problem was finally solved. This will depend on your requirements for the class and for particular children. However, a problem may finally be solved:

>when you have got an answer to the problem;
>when you have a solution to the problem;
>when you have a nice solution to the problem;
>when you have generalized or extended the problem;
>never!

CHAPTER 12   TEACHING PROBLEM SOLVING
- A START

1. INTRODUCTION

So far in this book we have largely been interested in the **doing** of problem solving. We've looked at lots of problems and shown how the concepts of heuristics and metacognition are helpful. We have given some space to scaffolding, the open ended questioning that is essential to help problem solvers over the rough spots. We now concentrate on the teaching of problem solving. Naturally, at the same time, we consider the learning of problem solving. The rest of this book then, is devoted to the philosophical reasons for introducing children to problem solving as well as the practicalities of putting problem solving into action in the every day classroom.

Five things need to be underlined at the start, however. The first is that this is our view of **teaching** problem solving at this moment. We believe that a lot more research needs to be undertaken to learn the best way for different children to assimilate problem solving and the best way for different teachers to explain problem solving to their classes. Undoubtedly there is still a lot we have to learn here.

The second thing that needs to be underlined is that there is no unique way to teach or to learn problem solving. Many different approaches have been observed and each teacher needs to find one which he or she is most comfortable with.

Thirdly, if you don't feel that you are a problem solver, then you may not want to jump in and attack problem solving head on. For you, a gentle introduction via small problems may be the best way to start. We'll say more about this later.

The fourth thing, you should bear in mind is that teaching mathematical problem solving is not very different from teaching language or any other part of the primary curriculum. The same skills of whole class and group teaching apply. Maybe the one key thing that you have to remember to do is to go through the problems you plan using **before** you get in front of the class. This is important because you need to be sure that the problem will do for you what you think it is going to do. We have observed many lessons where teachers expected a problem to go in one direction and it went in quite a different one. We'll come back to this later.

It is also important that you know how a problem comes out so that you know that it is the right level for your children. If you have a thorough knowledge of the problem, it will help you to provide good scaffolding for your class. Although be warned, sometimes you will

scaffold children away from using a correct solution which you hadn't thought of. With experience though, these times will be fewer.

Finally here, it's important to realise that problem solving has to be taught like anything else. Children will not become spontaneous problem solvers. You need to take them through the steps, stages and strategies and tell them what's going on. This way they will develop a vocabulary which will enable them to talk with you and with each other in reasonably precise terms. The vocabulary will also provide a means for them to think about what they're doing and monitor their own progress.

We summarise these five points below.

a.   Our view of best teaching practice is constantly changing.
b.   There is no unique way to teach or learn problem solving.
c.   You may want to introduce problem solving on a small scale.
d.   Teaching mathematical problem solving is similar to teaching other curriculum areas in the primary school.
e.   Problem solving has to be taught - it will not be learnt spontaneously.

Further Explorations

1.   (a) How have your views on problem solving changed while you've been working on this book?

     (b) In what ways do you think this change is likely to be reflected in your teaching?

2.   How would you teach problem solving? (Choose a particular class and think about your overall goals for the year as well as the way you would teach particular classes.)

3.   Refer back to a particular problem that we have used in this book. How could you use this to start problem solving "on a small scale"? What would you do to follow this up?

4.   (a) What do you think are the similarities between teaching mathematical problem solving and language?

     (b) What do you think are the differences in philosophy and practice between teaching mathematical problem solving and language?

     (c) What are the similarities and differences between teaching problem solving in mathematics and teaching problem solving in any other curriculum area?

     (d) What are the similarities and differences between teaching problem solving in mathematics and teaching any other part of mathematics?

5   (a) In your experience, do people become mathematical problem solvers spontaneously?

(b) Who is the best problem solver (in any context), that you know? What qualities make them good problem solvers? How did they become good problem solvers? (You may need to ask them in order to find out the answer to this question.)

2. WHY PROBLEM SOLVING?

It's important at the start that you understand why you are going to teach problem solving to your class. One reason, which is not necessarily a good one, is that it's in the curriculum or advocated by the NCTM in the USA. This does mean though, that someone somewhere believes that problem solving is important enough to recommend it to all teachers.

Below we list seven advantages that have been proposed for problem solving.

   (i)   It bases children's mathematical development on their current knowledge.
   (ii)   It is an interesting and enjoyable way to learn mathematics.
   (iii)   It is a way to learn mathematics with understanding.
   (iv)   It is a good way to practise mathematical skills learnt by other means.
   (v)   It encourages child communication and cooperation.
   (vi)   It puts children in the role of junior research mathematicians.
   (vii)   It generalizes to areas outside mathematics.

The first of these advantages links very nicely with Vygotsky and his zone of proximal development and with the constructivist theory of learning. Vygotsky noticed that children could perform tasks by themselves at a given cognitive level. However, when provided assistance by adults in the form of scaffolding, the same children were able to perform at a much higher cognitive level. The "region" between these two cognitive levels he called the children's **zone of proximal development**.

Constructivists believe that we all construct our knowledge of the world by interacting with it. Each piece of learning is built upon our previous knowledge. They believe that knowledge cannot be directly transferred from one person to another. Learning is not equivalent to filling an empty vase or writing on a clean blackboard. Rather learning is something which is constructed as the result of everyday experiences (both inside and outside the classroom).

Where does problem solving fit into these two theories of learning? The first thing to realise is that problem solving is very much a child-centred approach to learning. The emphasis is constantly on the child solving the problem in hand. This solving needs to be done in a supportive atmosphere with the teacher and other children assisting. Problem solving requires risk taking. Unless there is a supportive atmosphere, the children will not take risks.

The teacher then, is setting up supportive situations that allow the children to develop their understanding of mathematical concepts. The children construct their own meaning and this meaning is reinforced by bouncing it off the teacher and their peers.

As we have said, this is all done in a supportive atmosphere. The teacher uses scaffolding to extend the children to the limits of their zone of proximal development. Because there is no insistence on a **right** method, the children can produce a solution by whatever means is at their disposal. Hence one problem, if it is a suitably rich mathematical activity (we'll say more about these later), will cater for the needs of a variety of children with a range of cognitive abilities.

Problem solving starts with the child and with their knowledge and ability, and leads them to construct further knowledge. It encourages them to move toward the edge of their zone of proximal development.

The second advantage that we proposed was that problem solving is interesting and enjoyable. To reach this state may take time and practice on the part of the teacher but it does happen. It's unusual for a lecturer at a University to go into the next classroom to see what all the noise is about. But this actually happened when a problem solving group for secondary students was being held. The students were certainly making more noise than is usual in the hallowed halls of learning, hence the lecturer's concern. However, the students were all on-task and engaged in generating their solutions to a problem. Throughout our studies on problem solving we have found that girls and boys are equally interested in the tasks. In fact, girls seem to find problem solving more meaningful than the traditional teaching approach.

The same sort of behaviour has been observed in primary classrooms. We have evidence of a class of 7 and 8 year olds who were so intent on the problem in hand and their discussion of it with their peers, that they were totally oblivious of their teacher's request to bring the noise level down. Despite the noise, a great deal of active learning was in progress.

Problem solving doesn't always work like this, of course, but for many children it can be more interesting and engaging than the traditional approach. At least part of the reason for this is that the children seem to identify more with the problems that are being attempted. Another part is that the children are able to use their own approach to solving the problem. They do not have to slavishly follow an algorithm or method that they only partially comprehend. This does not mean that they never learn new approaches. By extending children to the limits of their zone of proximal development, higher level skills will be generated and will be applied more creatively.

The third claim for problem solving is that it leads to greater understanding. The reason for this is that children are given a great many opportunities to explore. On the odd occasion this will enable pupils to discover a mathematical idea for themselves. On many occasions exploring will sufficiently fertilise their cognitive regions that when a mathematical idea is put forward by the teacher, it will immediately take root and grow.

A problem called Silly Beasts illustrates this. Three animals are shown in Figure 1. Each animal has cards for the head, the body and the tail. A Silly Beast is one which consists of any head, any body and any tail. How many Silly Beasts can you make?

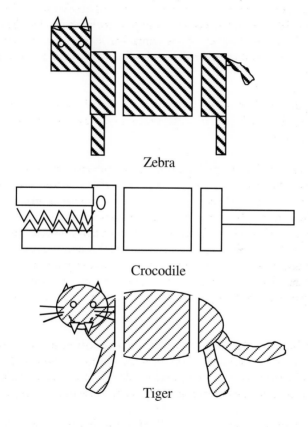

Zebra

Crocodile

Tiger

Silly Beasts

Figure 1

There are a number of ways of doing this. One which many children use is drawing up a list. Hopefully the list is drawn up systematically as in Figure 2.

head
body
tail
z
z
z
z
z
c
z
z
t
z
c
z
z
c
c
z
c
t
z
t
z
z
t
c
z
t
t
c
z
z
c
z
c
c
z
t
c
c
z

...

t
t
t

Here z = zebra part, c = crocodile part, t = tiger part

Figure 2

Now one teacher's aim in using this problem was to introduce the concept of a tree diagram. We show this in Figure 3.

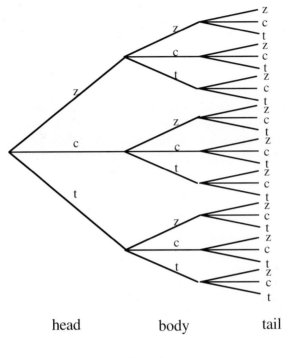

Figure 3

During the lesson none of the children came up with the idea of a tree diagram. However, when the concept was suggested by the teacher, it was readily accepted by many of the class and used in subsequent problems. The researchers observing this experience felt that this approach to tree diagrams led the children to a sound understanding of the concept of tree diagrams, of the need for tree diagrams and where and how tree diagrams could be employed.

Whether this understanding was deeper than could be achieved by a different teaching approach is open to question but it was certainly very effective for the class cited above. We have observed this phenomenon with the Silly Beast problem on more that one occasion. The reason we suspect that this problem works is that it is first of all an appealing situation for most children. They enjoy working with the concept and the cards. Second, there is the matter of "ownership". This is particularly true if children discover the concept of tree diagrams for themselves. But even if they don't they often have the feeling that they might have done if they had worked at the problem a little longer. Somehow all the bits fit together in their cognitive map and tree diagrams are suddenly a natural phenomenon that they have mastered, understood and are ready to use on another occasion.

Problem solving cannot be used to generate **all** the mathematical ideas and skills in the curriculum, largely because of the time factor involved. However, we believe there are few, if any, skills that cannot be introduced this way. There is some problem situation that can either stimulate children to invent the skill for themselves or will prepare the ground for effective learning and understanding.

It is worth noting here that, even if children are able to discover things for themselves, it does not necessarily mean they will remember them for ever. Discoveries can be forgotten over time. If the discovery is an important skill, it will need to be reinforced intermittently or it will be lost. There seems to be no research as yet on whether problem solving is more effective at aiding long-term retention than any other approach. Proponents of problem solving would claim that this is likely to be the case because of the understanding which accompanied the original learning.

The fourth advantage on our list was as a way to practice mathematical skills that have already been learnt. Problem solving can certainly provide an opportunity to reinforce and apply mathematical skills learnt previously. As such, problem solving can be a valuable tool for revision. However, there is evidence that children only use concepts in problem solving situations if they have thoroughly mastered the concepts. If scaffolding is used by the teacher, then this should not be a great difficulty and the use of the concept in a problem should lead to better use and recall on a future occasion.

If teachers use some of the ideas we propose later in Section 4, it should be clear that the fifth quality, that of communication and cooperation, can be advanced. In that section we advocate the use of cooperative groups in the course of problem solving lessons. The advantages of these groups have been extolled by many authors and we will not elaborate them further here.

We will note though, that communication is also effected in the reporting back sessions we propose at the conclusion of every problem solving lesson. As we note, reporting back should be more than just saying what answer the child has obtained. Communicating the methods that the children used is valuable to their learning because it aids their understanding. It also helps the rest of the class link together a variety of skills in different mathematical areas, when different groups find different ways of solving the problem.

Advantage number six is the matter of junior research mathematicians. Every discipline has its own culture and mores, and ways of approaching problems. Every discipline has the right to expect that children will be exposed to this side of the discipline. By putting them in situations where they have to find solutions, they can begin to experience the feelings and attitudes of research mathematicians. Hence they can gain a better appreciation of what mathematics is, how it works and what it is trying to achieve. This side of mathematics has not been seen traditionally in situations where the teacher tries to impart knowledge directly.

Finally on our list is the generalization factor. The research on this is not decisive. The hope is that by training children to solve problems in a mathematical environment, they will see how to tackle problems in real life. It does seem that making children aware of the way that moderately structured mathematics problems can be solved, they might begin to see how to tackle less well structured problems in every day life. As we said, though, there is no conclusive proof yet on this.

We have come across an interesting example, however, which suggests that problem solving can benefit the childrens' mathematics generally. One year we worked with a class of lower ability 14 year olds. They had four mathematics lessons a week and one of these was devoted solely to problem solving. The type of problem that they used can be seen by looking at the last set of Further Explorations in Chapter 1. So these problems were not extremely difficult or deep. In fact very often the class did three or four problems in a lesson.

About two-thirds of the way through the school year, all the 14 year olds in this particular school were given an examination. One exam was partly short answer questions (what is 15% of 320) and partly word problems. Only one of the five word problems was actually a "problem solving" problem.

It was clear from the results of the exam that the children in this class had done significantly well, especially in comparison with the other classes. We had the examination marks of almost all of the children in the school from the previous year. The children in the problem solving class increased their mark by about 7.5%. Only one of the other five classes improved their average. Individually almost all the children in this problem solving class had improved their mark over the previous year. This was the case with only half of the children in the other classes.

What we think happened was that during the problem solving class they had practised basic mathematical skills at their own pace. While they were problem solving they were also improving other skills because they were working on them at their own level and not being pushed along by the rest of the class or by the teacher's need to finish a topic.

In addition, almost all of the problems were word problems. As a result the children learned how to tackle such problems and had gained confidence that they could make progress on such problems. Hence when they met the word problems in the examination, they did not give up as easily as their peers in other classes had done.

The problem solving seemed to have increased the competence of the children in using basic skills and also seemed to have increased their confidence in their ability to tackle mathematical questions posed in a word form

Siemon and Booker sum up much of what we have said here in the following statement.

> "Problem solving recontextualises mathematics. It provides a rich background against which to interpret meaning, to apply basic ideas, to explore strategies, and to evaluate personal preferences. As such it is more likely to lead to insights into the processes of mathematical thinking than traditional processes. ... New mathematical ideas can grow out of appropriately posed mathematical problems."

As a postscript to this section it is important to point out that there are disadvantages to problem solving. Certainly problem solving is not perfect by any means.

Perhaps the biggest disadvantage is the one alluded to earlier. Using a problem solving approach to mathematics takes time. Various educators debate whether or not the whole of the curriculum can in fact be taught this way because of the time factor. It may come down to personal philosophy and teaching style. Certainly some teachers do teach each and every class in a year this way. They claim that time spent early on is well invested and that things become more time efficient as the year progresses. Other teachers claim this is not the case. They further feel that different children need to be taught in different ways and so it is important to vary the teaching approach. This problem is one which you will have to resolve for yourself and your solution may be a function of the children in your class, the school where you are teaching, as well as many other factors.

One other disadvantage of problem solving is that some teachers feel it is difficult to teach. This partly stems from the fact that they have had no experience with problem solving. Almost certainly, during their time at school, they would have been taught mathematics by the traditional method. Similarly, during their professional training they could not have met problem solving at all. Because the approach to problem solving in mathematics is similar to the approach used in other subject areas in the primary school, it should not be too difficult for teachers to understand how problem solving can be taught.

Another part of this difficulty of teaching problem solving is preparation. First of all, many teachers are unsure of where suitable problems can be found. We hope that we have given a large number of problems in this book that can be used at different levels in the school and which will be valuable for children with a range of abilities. Other books exist and we have listed some in the Reference section in the last chapter.

The second worry relating to preparation is that a child will come up with ideas that the teacher had not thought of before and that the teacher won't be able to handle these ideas. It may be that the teacher does not feel confident that they could decide whether or not the ideas are good ones or not. In situations like this, the teacher should first of all ask the child to develop their idea further. Treat the ideas as a conjecture. See where it leads. Is there a counterexample? The child may well be able to see the value of the idea very quickly if the right open questions are asked. Share the idea with other children. What do they think of it?

If the teacher can't settle it immediately, then there is no shame attached to that. The child can be told that it sounds an interesting idea and the teacher will think about it. This will buy some time so that the teacher can check with their colleagues and report back to the child at the next opportunity. Most difficulties of this type can generally be settled quickly. Occasionally though, the teacher may have to tell the child that they don't know whether the idea is right or not. On these occasions it is worth seeking help from a university, a teacher training institution or from somewhere else where there might be an expert.

Further Explorations

6. What do you know about Vygotsky and constructivism? Do you agree or disagree with Vygotsky or with the constructivist view of learning? Why?

7. (a) Have you seen interesting problem solving lessons?

    (b) Have you seen problem solving lessons which children clearly did not find interesting and enjoyable?

    (c) Why do you think the lesson turned out that way in (a) and (b)?

    (d) Repeat (a), (b) and (c) replacing "problem solving lessons" by "traditional maths lessons"?

8. Who was your most stimulating teacher? Why?

9. Can you suggest three reasons why the traditional approach to learning mathematics may lead to deeper understanding?

10. Think of a particular mathematical skill. Show how you could set up both a problem solving situation and a traditional mathematics situation to practice this skill.

11. (a) Why is it a good thing for children to cooperate and communicate?

    (b) What are the disadvantages of cooperation and communication?

    (c) Is there any value in providing situations in which children become junior research mathematicians?

(d) Can only very bright children gain anything by experiencing the junior research mathematician role?

12. What types of things, in your experience, generalise across subject boundaries?

3. BASIC LESSON FORMAT

Our experience suggests that a good lesson format consists of three phases. We've talked about them before. They are

a. Whole class - introduction.
b. Group work.
c. Whole class - report back.

Of course things are much more complicated than this. We'll start off by amplifying the list and then we'll indicate how the different phases may change to accommodate the children and their problem solving experience.

At the start of the lesson it is well worthwhile to get the whole class together and make sure that they are all at the same level. Then you can introduce the problem that you are going to use.

From here the children move into their groups (they may already be there) and start working together on the problem. The point of this phase of the lesson is to solve the problem while experiencing communication and collaboration. But it is here too, that most of the practising of problem solving skills and the application of mathematical skills will take place.

Most of the scaffolding by the teacher will be done during the group phases as it is here that the teacher moves from group to group helping where necessary and checking on progress.

The aim of the reporting back phase is not solely to see who has the right answer and who hasn't. Children should be encouraged to say what strategies they used and how these helped. Where possible the different strategies used by different groups should be compared. Do they all work equally well? Are some wrong? Are some "nicer" than others? Are two apparently different patterns actually the same?

During the reporting back stage you might also like to consider any generalizations or extensions of the problem.

This final phase of the lesson can be invaluable for seeing connections between different approaches and for appreciating what other groups have done. We have observed lessons where 5 year olds have reported back to a room of totally captivated classmates. Indeed the attention that the child reporter was accorded was better than that normally given to the teachers.

In a class of 13 year olds we have also seen quite weak children reporting back. By suitable encouragement from the teacher and their peers they have performed reasonably well. It is interesting to note that their peers were prepared to listen attentively to what they were saying. The whole process was taken very seriously and the children who were reporting back were given assistance when required.

On the other hand, we have observed a class of 12 year olds where the reporting back session was not at all successful. Little attention was paid to the child whose turn it was at the board. It was clear that this particular session was of no value at all. The main reason for this seemed to be that different groups were set different questions. Hence not all of the children had attempted the problem being reported to the class. Consequently some of the groups had no interest in what was being reported.

The three phases of the basic lesson might constitute the whole of a one hour period. Phase 1 could go for five minutes; phase 2 for forty minutes; and phase 3 for fifteen minutes. Naturally these times are not hard and fast and will vary as we consider the other variables in this process that we mention below.

The point that has to be made about this third phase is that it is as much a thinking and learning time as any of the other phases. Children are not there just to report their answers or to listen to other children's answers. It is important that the reporters **justify** what they have done. The rest of the class might be asked to challenge these justifications or help the reporters to see where they have made omissions or where things could be improved. Everybody should be weighing up the various reports and seeing how they fit together. Is one child's method really exactly the same as another's? How can this be justified.

Further Explorations

13. How does the three phase lesson format fit into Pólya's four phases of problem solving or the three steps of the "Read the problem ..." poem?

14. In what ways could you vary the three phase lesson format with a given class?

15. What is the aim of each of the phases in the basic lesson format?

16. During which of the three phases of the basic lesson format, should the teacher be using

    (i) heuristics; (ii) metacognition; (iii) scaffolding? Why?

17. (a) How many children would you have working together in groups?

   (b) How would you physically arrange the groups?

   (c) Would you let the children choose the groups themselves?

   (d) Would you allow the groups to be of mixed ability? Why?

◆ ◆ ◆ ◆

Now let's consider some variations on these themes and indicate how and why the variations could take place.

What we want to take into consideration is the specific needs of the children involved. So let's start in the junior primary school. Here children have a relatively short attention span. In particular this means that the whole class sections of problem solving lessons should be interesting for them and not take too long.

To make things interesting you should use rich mathematical activities. We'll say more about this later. Part of the answer is to keep them interested and entertained with demonstrations, pictures and stories. And part of the secret of success is to involve as many children as possible.

Young children's attention spans are particularly critical in the group work phase of the lesson. It is unlikely that groups of 5 year olds can profitably be kept working on tasks for very long. This means that the problem goals for this part of the lesson have to be well defined and limited. The older the children are, the longer they will be able to engage in their group work. Similarly, more can be expected of them during this phase.

During the group work phase of a lesson it may not be possible for the teacher to get to every single group. The most that can be done on some occasions is to get a quick feel for how the class as a whole is progressing. It may only be possible to engage in a limited amount of teaching. However, a quick eye over the groups will give the teacher a good idea of how they are coping. As a consequence, more teaching can be pursued during the report back phase.

If it is the teacher's observation that a large section of the class has a common problem, the report back session may be delayed. Instead, another whole class phase may be inserted so that the goals of the group phase may be achieved the second time around.

So, in the junior school, the first and third phases of the lesson may be considerably longer than the second phase. In addition, phases 1 and 2 may be repeated more than once before phase 3 is used.

Further Explorations

18. What other children may need a variation in the basic lesson format?

19. (a) What differences might you expect between the basic lesson format of a 5 year olds' class and a class of 15 year olds? Why?

    (b) What similarities might there be?

20. What are the advantages and disadvantages of different groups being set different questions?

21. What are the advantages and disadvantages of setting more than one problem for the group phase?

22. How would you overcome the differences in abilities between children?

In classes that have been streamed so that lower ability children have been grouped together in one class, we have observed the basic lesson format repeated several times in a mathematics period. So, for instance, with a group of weaker 14 year olds, the three phases may be repeated every 15 minutes or so. This seems to enable the children to keep concentrating and to be on-task for the whole period.

These children appear to enjoy taking an active part in the reporting back session, even if they do not necessarily fully understand how to solve the problem they are discussing. This may partly satisfy a need for attention, of course. But this basic desire can be turned to educational advantages. For instance, it can be used to reinforce the parts of the work that the children **do** know. And other children can give the reporter assistance which may well lead to learning on the part of both children.

Further Explorations

23. How would you decide which child from a given group should report back to the class?

24. Under what circumstances would you accept a child reporting back as follows: "the answer to the frog problem is 15".

25. Would you expect each group to report back a single solution - the group's solution? Or is the reporting back an individual affair?

4. GROUP WORK

The first question to ask of group work is why? What is it that you expect children to learn by working in groups that can't be learned as effectively in a whole class situation?

Groups give children an opportunity to work cooperatively with each other. They enable children to provide their own individual input into the solution of a given problem and so provide opportunities for the group to have a wider experience and see a greater variety of approaches to a problem than is the case for one individual. Groups encourage the sharing of ideas and the valuing of the contribution of each group member.

Groups also provide an opportunity for each member to monitor the ideas of others to say which ideas they think are good and which contain errors. One pair of 6 year olds that we observed consisted of a bright voluble child and an average-to-good but quiet child. The bright child did most of the talking and seemingly most of the work. However, every now and again the less able child quietly said "That's not 5" or "You miscounted there". While we believe that groups should generally have more interaction than this, the input of both was valuable here and the group product was better than either one or them would have been able to produce alone.

Groups also provide the opportunity for genuine learning and understanding that may not happen as easily in a whole class situation because children are unable to follow their ideas through to an end. In groups we have commonly seen situations where one child intuitively gets the feel for a problem but is not totally confident that their idea is correct. They will write down an answer but not be confident that their method of solution is correct. Then they try to explain what they have done to the rest of the group. During this explanation they seem to suddenly understand the situation and are able to complete the problem with confidence. Because children are allowed to speak to each other during group work, they are able to work through ideas aloud that they wouldn't be able to do in a traditional class. For some reason, this verbalisation is a strong tool in the learning process.

Above we have reported a positive situation but verbalising also seems to allow incorrect ideas to be discovered sooner too. It seems that putting ideas in to words provides an inbuilt mechanism for testing the ideas. Often an incorrect idea when verbalised, is easier to recognise than if it had not been brought into the open.

So cooperation, communication, creativity, learning and understanding should be expected from groups.

But groups don't just happen. By simply putting two, three, four or more people together around a table, cooperative productive behaviour will not just happen automatically. Group work has to be learned.

Further Explorations

26. What behaviour would you expect of groups? How would you encourage this behaviour?

27. How would you choose the members of a group? Why?

28. What would you do if you saw one member of a group consistently sitting quietly, working all alone?

As group work is a general teaching technique that is common across subject areas, we will not spend any further time discussing how to establish good cooperative behaviour. We will simply note that much has been written on this topic and refer you to Johnson, Johnson and Holubec.

We will however, make some general practical suggestions as to how to get maximum value out of groups. The first thing we want to talk about is group size. We would suggest that groups larger than four will not function well for mathematical problem solving. In such groups the social interactions become so complex that the groups tend not to work at all well.

Even groups of size four, tend to split up into two groups of two. This is largely because of the task and the physical set up. Because mathematical problem solving often requires children to write down their work, those who are sitting side by side tend to work together. This is because they can see the different pieces of paper they are each writing on. So in Figure 4, children A and B will tend to work with each other, as will children C and D.

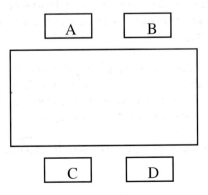

Figure 4

Similarly we have observed groups of three where one child has been ostracised, simply because of the physical set up. In Figure 5, the children were arranged for the convenience of a video camera. Children A and B worked together on a pen and paper task. Child C was left to work on their own. The fault was not child C's. In a later lesson, child A was in C's place. On that occasion B and C worked well together while child A was left out of the collaboration.

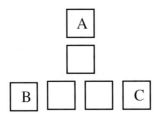

Figure 5

Further Explorations

29. Under what circumstances can groups of size three and four work well?

    Can groups of size five and above work successfully?

30. Devise an exercise in which three people can cooperate profitably.

The situation of Figure 5 became a truly cooperative situation when the task was not just a paper and pencil one. In a problem to do with towers, the children used multi-fix cubes. These were easily placed in the centres of their three desks. Each child then had the same easy access to the cubes and so was able to contribute to the group. Similar activities can be used with groups of size four with equal success.

If two is a good size for children it may be too small for teachers. With groups that small, it can take a teacher a long while to go round and work with every group in the class. Obviously four to a group makes the teacher's job easier.

Further Explorations

31. Which is more important, that children work in pairs or that teachers get to see each group in a lesson?

32. Are there alternative strategies that teachers can use in order to get round all groups?

Some teachers prefer to have groups of size four because they feel they can do them more justice (i.e. service them more often), than smaller groups. On the other hand, some teachers in such situations realise they can't work with every group in a lesson. They plan to see each group over two lessons or to see each group an equal number of times over the period of a week.

Another strategy is to have key groups. These groups are about average in ability. The teacher makes sure they visit these groups regularly. If these groups are working well and making progress, then it's almost certain that higher ability groups will be doing well and will not require so much of their attention. If the key groups appear to be in trouble, though, then weaker groups will certainly have their backs against the wall. When there is such a difficulty, these teachers run a whole class session with a view to overcoming the difficulties together. After some whole class discussion, the groups can go back to work again.

Further Exploration

33. What are the aims of the group parts of a mathematical problem solving lesson? Can these aims be achieved in a whole class setting? Why? Why not?

5. SCAFFOLDING

Having got the classroom organised with groups running well and using whole class, group work and reporting back sessions, what now? The next thing to consider is the teacher's interaction with the children. We've talked about scaffolding before. It's the kind of questioning and demeanour that you use to get children around barriers and to coach them to a successful conclusion. If anything, this aspect of teaching is the most important. It may be the least understood.

Take a step back for a moment. The difference between taking a problem solving approach to teaching and using the old approach is that it is child centred. The aim is to build on what the child knows. The aim is not to show how clever the teacher is and to show how much the teacher knows. Rather it is to help the child make sense of the world through careful coaching.

So every opportunity should be given to allow the children to explore and create and construct their own learning. All the while though, the children are being carefully guided to knowledge by the teacher, by scaffolding.

The underlying philosophy which guides the questions you ask the children is an open one. What do you think is the way to tackle this problem? Why do you believe that? Why do you think the answer is three? Somebody else has a different reason. Which is right? Why?

Forget for the moment that this book has anything to do with mathematics. What sort of questioning do you use in language lessons? How do you elicit answers during reading and writing? The basic philosophy there is the basic philosophy in problem solving in mathematics. This is in fact why some primary teachers enjoy teaching problem solving - it's just the way they teach almost everything else. For so long in the primary school the teaching of mathematics has been totally different from the teaching of everything else. Problem solving is a way of bringing all your teaching together.

Further Explorations

34. A group is working well. They are on-task. You move to their table. How long do you stand there before you say anything? What is the first thing you say and why?

35. A group is working badly. They are off-task. You move to their table. How long do you stand there before you say anything? What is the first thing you say and why?

36. How do you respond when a group has found the solution to a problem? Do you respond in the same way whether the answer is right or wrong? Should you respond in the same way?

◆ ◆ ◆

Writing about scaffolding is a bit like writing about how to learn to ride a biker. The point is that learning to ride a bike is best done by getting on a bike and trying. Similarly scaffolding is best learnt by doing it or by watching others do it. It is also a skill that everyone can learn.

Having said that though, there are a few things that are worth saying about scaffolding. First of all the main reason for scaffolding is to help children over barriers. Barriers to problem solving may be of three types - cognitive, metacognitive or affective.

A **cognitive barrier** may exist because the child doesn't know a piece of mathematics, a skill, that can be used in the present situation. Alternatively, they know the skill but have forgotten it or don't realise that it is relevant in the current situation. In the first situation it may be necessary to teach the skill before the child can do the problem. Normally you would not expect children to tackle a problem unless you thought they had the necessary skills. (However, there are times when you want to introduce a skill via a problem. We talked about this earlier with respect to tree diagrams.) In the case where a relevant known skill is required, the teacher can just say "why not use long division" but this won't help the child when they are in a similar position in the future. Try to lead them to think about what area of maths it is and what skills they might need. "Does this look like a situation you've seen before?" What did you do then?" "Do you have to combine these numbers somehow": What might be an appropriate way of doing that? … Why? Has that got you the right answer?"

A **metacognitive barrier** may exist because the child has become absorbed in a method which is not leading anywhere. The child has got onto a single track and is unable to see that this is not leading anywhere. At this point the teacher could ask "How is it going? What do you think of this approach? Where do you hope to get this way? What other strategies could you try?" By using a series of questions of this type, the teacher may be able to help the child overcome the current metacognitive barrier.

Finally, an **affective barrier** is one caused by an affective difficulty. These can be the most difficult to provide scaffolding for. It may be that the child is having difficulty with the context of the problem. We once asked a problem about a cat called Dog. (One of us actually has a cat that our children called Dog!) One child was totally unable to start on this problem because he thought that that was a stupid name for a cat. When we reworded the problem the child happily solved it.

Children can also believe that if a problem can't be solved in 10 minutes, then it simply cannot be solved. Affective scaffolding is requited to coax them round that hurdle.

Further Explorations

37. Can scaffolding fail? Why?

38. Should you never, under any circumstances tell children an answer?

It is worth noting that we have observed some excellent scaffolding by teachers which has been totally ignored by the group being scaffolded. There may be at least two possible explanations for this. First, the children are so convinced that their method is correct that it may be impossible to convince them of their error for some time. In this instance, affective scaffolding is required but it may be best to let the children begin to see that they are not getting anywhere before trying again. Of course, one of the difficulties here is that the children may be right. Their method may work. We have been in situations like this where we thought that a method wasn't going to work. We hadn't seen the method used before on that particular problem. Our children ignored our scaffolding and eventually solved the problem. So if the difficulty is related to method and the teacher is unsure of whether it will work or not, then it is best to stand back and wait for a while.

Another reason that the scaffolding might not be accepted is that the children might not have understood what the teacher said. There is no doubt that this situation can occur, perhaps because the teacher's language is somehow too sophisticated or technical. One way round such difficulties is to ask some child from another group to talk to the children who are not making progress. Incidentally, this language difference between adults and children is one reason why reporting back sessions can be so successful. Children interact at a different level than do children and teachers, and children are often more comfortable in the former situations.

6. RICH MATHEMATICAL ACTIVITIES

In the early 1980s when a great deal of problem solving began to be used, the theorists believed that all you had to do was to give teachers "rich mathematical activities". They believed that in teachers' hand these would inevitably lead to good problem solving on the part of children. This problem solving would simultaneously provide good mathematical learning.

Very few people believe now that rich mathematical activities are the end of problem solving pedagogy. However, they are the beginning. Without a good problem there can be no good problem solving. So what is a good problem? What is a rich mathematical activity?

For a start, any problem you give to your class has to have appeal to them. Teddy Bears are a great subject for 6 and 7 year olds. You have to have a great deal more teaching skill to use a problem about Teddy Bears with 16 and 17 year olds. The topic of the problem has to be appropriate and engaging.

Further Explorations

39. (a) Make a list of the topics which you think will appeal and be of interest to a group of 5 year olds.

   (b) Repeat (a) for a class of 8 year olds.

   (c) Repeat (a) for a class of 11 year olds.

40. What topics will appeal to both 5 year olds and 11 year olds?

◆ ◆ ◆ ◆

We are fairly egocentric. You can usually catch our attention and interest by building us into the conversation. So it is with children. They will be fascinated and engaged by questions in which they play a role. We've hinted at this elsewhere when we have asked you to rephrase a question using some children you know as participants.

Animals are also appealing, especially big ones and very small ones. You can usually succeed with dinosaurs and elephants. Rabbits and other small cuddly animals generally do well too.

If there is a choice between a reasonably real (if a little far-fetched) context and an abstract one, choose the real one every time.

So we think you've probably got the idea of making the context interesting and relevant. Now let's think about the problem. What qualities does the actual problem have to have?

First, it is not a good problem if it is no challenge. Remember the problem of how many legs have three sheep? A good problem for 5 year olds. Once you know anything about multiplication it's no problem at all. But for 5 year olds it requires a choice of strategy. Then it probably requires some counting and counting to the limit of their counting ability.

Second, a rich mathematical activity will fall to a variety of attacks. If there is more than one way to skin a rabbit, there is more than one method of solution for a rich mathematical activity. The importance of this range of solution methods is that it gives many children the opportunity to produce a solution. A problem that will fall to an organised list, or table and a nifty piece of algebra will be accessible to almost all the children in the class. We have covered one of the basic laws of learning. All children should have some success!

But there's more to it than just getting all children to be successful. In the reflection-reporting back session at the end of the lesson, the different approaches should appear. At this stage, using an open approach, you, as the teacher, should be able to link the different methods. You should be able to show the relation between them and use the opportunity to teach the less able children the more sophisticated method. The more able children should benefit by seeing and understanding the links between all the methods proposed.

Finally, a rich mathematical activity should not just be a one-off closed task. There should be an opportunity to extend or to generalize the problem. While the weaker children are struggling with the activity, the more able children can be challenged to take the problem further. In fact this could be the challenge to your able children with every problem. When they have solved the problem, they have to generalise or extend it. (Another useful devise is to ask them to invent another problem similar to the one they have just solved.)

It is, of course, important for all children to have the opportunity to generalize and extend at some stage. However, weaker children will often be having sufficient challenges with the problem as it stands without having to worry about generalizations and extensions.

Further Explorations

41. Take three of the problems from anywhere in this book. Say why they are rich mathematical activities or say why they are not.

42. Find a problem of your own. Why is it a rich mathematical activity?

43. For the problems in the last two Explorations, are they rich mathematical activities for all children? Are they only rich mathematical activities for children of a certain age, or background, or gender or ...?

7. WHERE NOW?

There is only one more chapter after this. This includes a selection of sample lessons that you might like to try as they stand or adapt them and try them. These lesson plans are just one-off ideas to get you started. They are a way of testing the waters and a means for you to gain confidence. We suggest you start small like this and become more ambitious as you go. Our ideal is that you eventually incorporate aspects of problem solving into **all** of your mathematics teaching. With experience you will see how to do this. If you can't, the publisher has our address. Write us a letter.

Unfortunately the lesson plans are not foolproof. Rich mathematical activities can be subverted. The first trap for young players is to go into a lesson unprepared. Whatever you do, tackle the problem by yourself before you go into the classroom. Do this well ahead of time. When you are convinced that you know how to do it, write it out in full. The first few times you might write the problem up as a case study as we did in Chapter 9.

If you are not happy with your solution try to solve the problem again. If you are happy with it, try to convince a friend. Only when you have worked over the problem in this way should you use it with your class.

But then there is the second thing that you need to do. That is to think like a child. What traps did the problem have for you? What traps will it have for your children? How did you get over your difficulties? How will you help them get over their difficulties?

Now give the lessons a trial run in your head.

Further Explorations

44. Go through the problems in the lesson plans of the next chapter.

    Write them all up as case studies. Are there many ways of solving these problems?

45. In the problems of the next chapter, what traps did they have for you? How did you avoid these traps?

    What difficulties do you think the problems will have for your children? How will you help them overcome these difficulties?

◆ ◆ ◆ ◆

The last section of this book is a reading list. This list contains ideas about educational philosophy, ideas about problem solving and practical resources that you can use in your classroom. You don't need to read them all at once but you should try to read something now and again to keep your pedagogical skills growing.

Good luck with your teaching! And we're serious about you writing to us.

8. CHAPTER SUMMARY

In this chapter we give suggestions on ways to start problem solving teaching. Our basic philosophy is that

our view of best teaching practice is constantly changing;
there is no unique way to teach or learn problem solving;
you may want to introduce problem solving on a small scale;
teaching problem solving is similar to teaching other curriculum areas in the primary school;
problem solving has to be taught - it will not be learnt spontaneously.

We then give the following advantages for problem solving:

it bases children's mathematical development on their current knowledge;
it is an interesting and enjoyable way to learn mathematics;
it is a way to learn mathematics with understanding;
it is a good way to practice mathematical skills learnt by other means
it encourages class communication and cooperation;
it puts children in the role of junior research mathematician;
it generalizes to areas outside mathematics.

We amplify the basic lesson format for problem solving that we gave in Chapter 3. This is

whole class - introduction;
group work;
whole class - report back.

We then talk about the basic aspects of group work and scaffolding, the positive interaction required to help children overcome difficulties. All of problem solving depends on the tasks that are used, so we talk about rich mathematical activities.

CHAPTER 13   SAMPLE LESSONS

1. SOCKS

Area: Algebra   **Age: 5-6 yrs**

Achievement Objective
Make and describe repeating sequential patterns.
Continue a repeating sequential pattern.

INTRODUCTION

The teacher has pegged coloured cut out "socks" on a string line. The children are encouraged to read the pattern, and predict (e.g. red, blue, red, blue) what colour the next sock will be. The teacher then continues the pattern to allow the children to check their prediction.

Individual children are invited to construct a sock pattern with the class reading and predicting.

The teacher presents the problem for the whole class to solve. Using an overhead projector, string, shaped beads and cubes, the teacher constructs a pattern representing a necklace, e.g. square, circle, circle, square or square, oval, circle etc.

"Sally's necklace has been broken. Can you help her by showing where the beads should be threaded?"

The teacher encourages the children to 'read' the bead pattern and asks children to suggest in which order the spare beads should be threaded.

Some helpful questions:

- How many parts are there to this pattern?
- Where does the pattern start? Where does it finish? Where does it start again?
- What will come next? How do you know?

The class are given the following problems to solve.

The clowns in the circus are juggling. The balls make a pattern but the last three have lost their juggling balls. Can you show them juggling - remember to keep the pattern going.

Mr Blink, the photographer, has come to Sunny Days school and all the classes are to have their photos taken. Mr Blink sorts the children into line. Can you see the pattern he is using? Who will come next? Carry Mr Blinks' pattern on.

The teacher provides paper and pens, coloured rods of varying lengths, counters and cubes.

CONCLUSION

The children come together to share their solutions.

2. BOXES

Area: Geometry Age: 5-6 yrs

Achievement Objective
Identify and describe, in their own language, the following 2-dimensional and 3–dimensional shapes: triangle, square, oblong, circle, oval, pentagon, hexagon, diamond, box, cylinder and sphere.

Teacher reads a story like "My Cat Likes to Hide in Boxes".
Talk about things that come in boxes and build up a language chart   "...... come in boxes".
Challenge the children to construct boxes. Provide cardboard, scissors and sticky tape.

CONCLUSION

When completed the "boxes" are brought to a sharing session. The children are encouraged to talk about how they made their box with the teacher emphasising the shapes that children used in order to make a box.

These shapes could be recorded on a chart.

"My box has two squares and four rectangles." etc.

This lesson could be followed the next day with the children taking real boxes apart and compare the shapes with their own box shapes.

3. CHUCKLES THE CLOWN

Area: Number   Age: 5-6 yrs.

Achievement Objective
Make up, tell and record number stories.

INTRODUCTION

The teacher shares a circus story or poem.

The teacher shows a coloured picture of a clown. "This is Chuckles, he is a world famous clown. He works in a circus with other clowns. Can you tell me what sorts of things clowns might do? What do clowns like to wear? In the circus where Chuckles works there are three clowns. How many noses will there be? How may floppy clown shoes?"

The teacher has made available paper and crayons, bottle tops, cardboard clowns, coloured rods.

The children are free to solve the problem in any way they choose.

SHARING TIME

Ensure the children are able to easily see the person who is speaking. Encourage different children to demonstrate the way they found an answer. Name each strategy as it is used. These strategies could be recorded with a picture as a visual cue, and referred to at other times.

4. THE LADYBIRD AND THE CATERPILLAR

Area: Algebra   Age: 7-8 yrs

Achievement objective:
Continue a sequential pattern and describe a rule for this.

INTRODUCTION

The class plays guess the rule. A number is given to the teacher who uses a "secret" rule to change it into a second number. These numbers are recorded on the board. Children try to guess the rule.

The teacher reads the following problem which is also recorded in a way that is visible to the whole class.

A ladybird and a caterpillar are having a race up a flowerstalk towards a red tulip. The flowerstalk is 32cm long. On the first day both the ladybird and the caterpillar have moved 1cm. By the second day the ladybird has moved 6cm and the caterpillar has crawled 2cm. By the third day the ladybird has moved 11cm and the caterpillar has crawled 4cm. By the fourth day the ladybird has travelled 16cm and the caterpillar has moved 8cm. If the creatures continue moving in this way who will win the race?

The following questions might be asked:

- What is the problem asking you?
- What is happening?
- What information are we given?
- What does it mean when it says "the creatures continue moving in this way"?
- How can we best solve this problem?

After a general discussion about possible strategies the teacher shows cut outs of a ladybird, a caterpillar and a coloured flower.

The teacher rolls out a sheet of paper which is marked from 0 to 32. The ladybird and the caterpillar are placed at 0 and the flower at the opposite end.

Children are asked to make predictions based on the information given. As the "characters" are moved, the teacher circles in red the distance they have travelled. The children are questioned:

- Where was the ladybird on Monday?
- How much further was it on Tuesday? on Wednesday? etc.
- Can you see a number pattern?

When the "race" is finished and a solution found, the class may discuss the strategy they have used. The teacher then leads into modelling "make a table" by asking for ways that they could best keep track of the information.

The teacher constructs a table and with assistance from the children completes the table and discusses the pattern.

The following problem is then given:

Hone and Pete are collecting magic cards. On Monday they both had 3. On Tuesday Hone got 4 and Pete got 6. On Wednesday Hone got 5 and Pete got 9. If the boys keep getting magic cards in the same way, how many cards will Pete get when Hone gets 9?

The teacher questions to make sure the children understand the question and the information given. In pairs the children are asked to solve the problem.

CONCLUSION

The children are encouraged to discuss and show their solutions.

5. THREE BILLY GOATS GRUFF

Area: *   **Age:** 7-8 yrs.

Achievement Objective:

INTRODUCTION

The teacher retells the story of the Three Billy Goats Gruff. The children are given parts and they act out the story as it is told. At the end of the story the teacher asks "In what order did the goats cross the bridge?"

The teacher draws this. "Could they have crossed the bridge in any other order?" The children act out the different combinations that could be used.

The teacher points out that she has become muddled and can't remember which order everyone crossed in. "How can we keep track?"

All suggestions should be discussed. The teacher returns to the earlier picture. "Could I use pictures to keep track?" The teacher, with the class assisting, completes the pictures.

This could lead to a further discussion about keeping track and use of time. On an overhead projector the teacher uses 3 different sized counters to represent Big, Middle and Little sized goats. The teacher demonstrates using an initial letter for each counter and begins recording possible combinations suggested by the class. The class are then asked to complete the list for themselves.

When they return to the mat the combinations are discussed and recorded. Once again the teacher brings their attention to the idea of keeping track and use of time.

The teacher introduces the idea of writing the list in an ordered way, (see Chapter 2 The Pictures) and the class are asked to rearrange their lists in an ordered way.

Answers are compared and discussed.

6. A STEAMY JUNGLE

Area: Number   Age: 7-8 yrs.

Achievement Objective:
Write and solve story problems which involve whole numbers, using addition, subtraction, multiplication or division.

INTRODUCTION

The teacher revises the "Steps to Solving Problems" which is recorded on a large chart.

The teacher displays the following problem:

In a damp steamy jungle there is a large muddy waterhole. Gathered around the water can be seen 3 pairs of elephants, 2 pairs of zebras, 2 pairs of tigers and a pair of snakes. BANG!! A gun explodes. All of the animals disappear. How many footprints are left in the mud?

The class discusses the problem. The teacher asks

- What are the important parts of the problem?
  (These are underlined in red felt pen)
- What happens in the problem?
- What are we asked to find out?

The children work in pairs to solve the problem. The teacher has made available pencil and paper, a variety of equipment including plastic animals and calculators.

When the children feel they have completed the problem they are directed to the class chart to check that they have covered all the steps to solving a problem, they then write a similar problem of their own. They must have a solution to their own problem before they ask someone else to solve it. These problems may later be published and made available to the whole class.

CONCLUSION

The teacher and class discuss the various strategies used to solve the problem.

Further Explanation

1. Trial the lessons from this Chapter.

    What were the good and bad points? How would you change the lesson next time?

2. Consider the following problem.

    How high would a stack of one million sheets of paper be?

    Plan a lesson for 11-12 year old children around this question. What would you hope to achieve in such a lesson?

3. Build a small stack of blocks on a rectangular plan. Note the shape from the "front", the "side" and the "top". The problem for the children is, given these three views, to construct the original stack of blocks. You might also ask what is the least number of blocks that would fit the three views and what is the largest such number.

    Plan and trial the lesson.

    What are your achievement objectives here?

4. Using any of the problems in this book, plan and trial three lessons for 9 and 10 year olds and three lessons for 11 and 12 year olds.

    What were the good and bad points of the lessons? How would would you extend the problems both for the more able students and for the average student.

5. Find some problems for yourself that are not in this book. Use them as the basis for problem solving lessons. Reflect on the results of those lessons.

6. What heuristics did the children use in the lessons above?

   What scaffolding did you provide? Was it always effective?

7. Having had some experience, what do you think of Pólya's four-step model? Would you alter it in any way?

   Reconsider the experiment, conjecture, etc model in the same way.

8. Did you use the three step lesson plan for your lessons? Why? Why not?

   How would you modify what we said here about that lesson format?

9. How did the groups work in your class?

10. Did you use a reporting back plan?

    How did that work?

FURTHER READING

1. PROBLEM SOLVING - THEORY

Krulik, S. (Ed.).   Problem Solving in School Mathematics. Reston, VA: NCTM.

Neyland, J. (Ed). (1994 and 1995)
                                 Mathematics Education - A Handbook for Teachers (Volume 1, 1994; Volume 2, 1995). Wellington, N.Z.: Wellington College of Education.

National Council of Teachers of Mathematics, (1980).
                                 An Agenda For Action. Reston VA: NCTM.

Pólya, G. (1945).   How To Solve It. Princeton, NJ: Princeton University Press.

Pólya, G. (1962, 1965).
                                 Mathematical Discovery (Volume 1, 1962; Volume 2, 1965). Princeton, NJ: Princeton University Press.

Schoenfeld, A.H. (1992).
                                 Learning to Think Mathematically: Problem Solving, Metacognition and Sense Making in Mathematics. In Grouws, D.A. (Ed). Handbook of Research on Mathematics Teaching and Learning, pp.334-370. New York: MacMillan.

2. PROBLEM SOLVING - RESOURCES.

Bird, M. (1986).   Mathematics with Seven and Eight Year Olds, Mathematical Association, London.

Bird, M. (1986).   Mathematics with Eight and Nine Year Olds, Mathematical Association, London.

Bird, M. (1986).   Mathematics with Nine and Ten Year Olds, Mathematical Association, London.

Bird, M. (1986).   Mathematics with Ten and Eleven Year Olds,
                             Mathematical Association, London.
Bird, M. (1991).   Mathematics for Young Children, Routledge.

Holton, D.A. and Thomas, B. (1998).
                             Teaching Problem Solving: A Resource for Primary
                             Teachers. Learning Media, Wellington, New Zealand.

Stacey, K. and Groves, S. (1985).
                             Strategies In Problem Solving. Camberwell, Victoria:
                             Latitude Publications.

Stokes, B. (1995).   Stretch, Bend and Boggle. Hamilton, NZ: Waikato
                             Education Centre.

3. FURTHER READING

Berk, L.E. and Winsler, A. (1995).
                             Scaffolding Children's Learning: Vygotsky and Early
                             Childhood Education. Washington, D.C: National
                             Association for the Education of Young Children.

Johnson, D.W., Johnson, R.J., Holubec, E.J. and Roy, P. (1984).
                             Circles of Learning: Cooperation in the Classroom.
                             USA: ASCD.

von Glasersfeld, E. (1990)
                             An exposition of constructivism: Why some like it rad-
                             ical. In Davis, R.B., Maha, C.A. and Noddings, N.
                             (Eds.) Constructivist views on the teaching and learn-
                             ing of mathematics, Journal for Research in
                             Mathematics Education, Monograph Number 4.
                             Reston, VA: National Council of Teachers in
                             Mathematics.

Vygotsky, L.S. (1962).
                             Thought and Language. Cambridge: MIT Press and
                             Wiley.

INDEX